VOGUE & BUTTERICK'S
CRAFT PROJECTS

VOGUE & BUTTERICK'S
CRAFT PROJECTS

Introduction by Nancy Fleming

A FIRESIDE BOOK
Published by **SIMON & SCHUSTER INC.**
New York   London   Toronto   Sydney   Tokyo   Singapore

F

FIRESIDE
SIMON & SCHUSTER, INC.
Rockefeller Center
1230 Avenue of the Americas
New York, New York 10020

Copyright© 1994 by The Butterick Company, Inc.

Editor Patricia Malcolm
Editorial Production Manager Barbara Machtiger
Contributing Writers Rosalie Cooke, Jacquelyn Smyth
Technical Editor Patricia Richards
Editorial Assistant Lila Chin
Patternmaker Crystal McDougald

President and Chief Executive Officer John E. Lehmann
Publisher Art Joinnides
Senior Vice President, Editorial Director Patricia Perry
Vice President, Creative Director Sidney Escowitz
Fashion Director Cindy Rose
Technical Director Janet DuBane
Art Directors/Cover Design Jeffrey Engel, Joe Vior
Production Manager Caroline Testaverde-Politi
Technical Consultant Joanne Pugh-Gannon
Marketing Consultant Mike Shatzkin

Book development, design and production provided by BMR, Corte Madera, CA
Publishing Director Jack Jennings
Project Manager Jo Lynn Taylor
Electronic Page Layout Emily Douglas, Micaela Carr

Printed in the U.S.A. by R.R. Donnelly
10 9 8 7 6 5 4 3 2 1
Library of Congress Cataloging in Publication Data
Vogue & Butterick's Craft Projects/Introduction by Nancy Fleming.
p.   cm.
"Fireside book." Includes index.
ISBN: 0-671-88873-0
1. Patchwork–Patterns. 2. Appliqué–Patterns. 3. Machine sewing.
I. Vogue & Butterick Patterns. II. Title: Vogue & Butterick's Craft Projects.
TT835.V62 1994   94-1209
746.46–dc20   CIP

To Our Readers

Dear Reader,

Home sewers have many bonds, but perhaps the strongest is our desire for creativity. As a school girl, I made my clothes out of necessity, since my allowance and taste in fashionable trends were not a good match. Soon I discovered the pride we all feel when responding to a compliment with the phrase, "Thank you, I made it myself!" Not only could I duplicate the looks I saw in fashion magazines, I could also individualize my wardrobe by choosing fabrics, colors, and accessories that worked best for me.

Sewing changed my life dramatically when I won the Miss America title using sewing for my talent presentation. The last line in my commentary was, "Have basic dress, will travel." This sign-off turned out to be extremely prophetic!

Through the years, my interest and skill in sewing have remained a way to express myself, whether sewing for my family, my television career wardrobe, my home, or crafts for gifts or charity bazaars.

The television series *Sewing Today* allows me an opportunity to combine many years of experience as a television show host and a home sewer. It is an exciting chance to meet the world's top designers in fashion, home decorating, and crafts. We hope to inspire you with the very best in contemporary design. Through the series and this book we also intend to increase sewing expertise with sewing information that utilizes professional techniques and the marvelous technology available today for home use. It's great fun for me to continue to learn more about something that has brought so much pleasure into my life, and it is an added joy to be able to share this creative process with you.

Happy Sewing,

Nancy Fleming

Contents

CHAPTER 1

Presenting Patchwork and Quilting

Traditionally, quilters spent many hours cutting, piecing, and quilting to create exquisite quilts and coverlets to bring warmth to their homes and families. Today's quilter cherishes the same values but has much less time to invest in the painstaking handwork that was once necessary to achieve these ends. Sewing machines, rotary cutters, fusibles, and a myriad of modern quilting products allow the contemporary quilter the luxury of turning out beautiful pieces in a fraction of the time. In this chapter, we offer a variety of familiar designs and time-honored techniques with a fresh, new twist for sewing today.

The Basics

Each project in this chapter highlights a different procedure used to create beautiful patchwork and quilts. To ensure successful results and years of enjoyment from your work, take time to familiarize or reacquaint yourself with the material in this section.

Tools of the Trade

Using quality materials and equipment will make your quilting project proceed more smoothly and accurately. Always buy the best you can afford—you will be pleased with the results of your time and investment.

CUTTING

Sharp dressmaking shears. They should be at least 8" (20.5 cm) long. Shop for quality and comfort.

Rotary cutter and self-healing cutting mat. Allows accurate cutting of up to 12 layers of fabric at once (see On the Cutting Edge, page 14). Choose a cutter with a comfortable handle to minimize fatigue and with a safety shield or retractable blade. Use a mat with a grid at least 22" (56 cm) wide.

Small, sharp-pointed embroidery scissors. For snipping threads, clipping seams, and slipping fabric under the presser foot.

Appliqué scissors. Flange allows close trimming of appliqués without cutting into background fabric.

Craft knife or paper scissors. Use for cutting templates.

MEASURING

Clear acrylic rulers with marked grids. Use for measuring and as a straightedge for rotary cutting. Grids and numbers marked on the underside help prevent fabric slippage. The most versatile size is 6" x 24" (15 cm x 61 cm).

Triangular and shaped rulers. Useful for marking triangles, curved, or angled patches.

MARKING

Tailor's chalk and chalk markers. Use for marking quilting lines on a completed quilt top.

Disappearing markers. Pens or pencils that are either water-soluble or will gradually fade over a short period of time.

Hard lead pencil. Use to trace template outlines onto fabric and mark quilting lines onto quilt top.

Pencil eraser. Removes pencil marks from cotton fabric.

TEMPLATES

Cardboard or template plastic. Make your own templates by tracing patterns directly onto tracing paper. Glue the tracing paper to cardboard and cut out. Patterns can be drawn onto graph paper and used in the same way, or they can be traced directly onto template plastic and cut out.

Purchased templates. These are available for many patchwork patterns and quilting designs.

NEEDLES AND PINS

Machine needles. For cotton fabrics, use size 80/12. If working with other fabrics, consult your machine manual.

Quilting needles or betweens. Use for hand quilting. Select sizes 8, 9, or 10.

Long straight pins with plastic heads. They are easy to handle when working through several layers, and their colored heads make locating them simple.

Safety pins. Use to baste quilt layers together in place of thread basting. Choose sizes 1 or 2. Brass pins won't rust and mark fabrics.

THREADS

One-hundred-percent cotton or cotton-wrapped polyester. Use for piecing, quilt construction, and machine quilting. If possible, try to match thread content to fabric content.

Quilting thread. Stronger than sewing thread, this is used for machine and hand quilting. Waxing will eliminate knotting and make the thread stronger.

Decorative threads. Choose metallic or rayon threads; or you may prefer to use transparent nylon thread for machine quilting.

STABILIZERS

In order to retain the shapes of appliqués and get sharp points, smooth curves, and perfect edges, a backing must be applied to the appliqué fabric. Select freezer paper, fusible web, or a water-soluble stabilizer to meet the needs of your project.

HAND QUILTING

Quilting hoop or frame. Holds fabric taut to achieve straighter, smaller stitches.

Thimbles. Use a flat-topped metal thimble on the middle finger of the quilting hand. You may wish to use a thimble or finger guard on the hand below the quilt.

MACHINE SEWING

Make certain your sewing machine has been oiled and is in good working order. Use a new needle for each project. Various feet or attachments are useful for patchwork and quilting projects (see Performing Feet, below). Some of the projects in this chapter make use of decorative machine stitching. Consult your machine manual for setup. If your machine does not have this capability, work the decorative stitching by hand.

PRESSING

Press all fabrics and seams at every step of the cutting, patchwork, and quilting process.

PERFORMING FEET

Adding appropriate presser feet to your sewing machine will help make patchwork and quilting easier, more precise, and assure successful results.

PATCHWORK FOOT aligns edge of foot with fabric edge for accurate 1/4" (6 mm) seams.

WALKING FOOT prevents layers from creeping and helps feed them evenly.

EMBROIDERY FEET have open toes for visibility. APPLIQUÉ FEET have smooth-feeding soles.

QUILTING FOOT has a large open space for easy guidance and visibility.

COLOR CONFIDENCE

TIPS FOR CHOOSING FABRIC

- View fabrics in natural daylight.
- Select a variety of print sizes. Balance bold prints with smaller prints and solids. Let color be the unifying theme.
- Small prints will look like solids from a distance, so take this into consideration in planning. Squinting at the fabric will give you an idea of how it will appear.
- Plaids and stripes add interest. Be sure to keep the lines straight when cutting and piecing.

- Plan carefully when cutting fabrics with directional designs. These often work well when used for borders.
- Decide on the mood you want your quilt to convey. Select one fabric you love that fits the feeling you want to convey and build the other fabrics around it. Lay fabrics beside each other to see their interplay.
- Cool colors (blues and greens) recede, while warm colors (reds and yellows) come forward. To achieve design balance, use a few

more cool-colored fabrics than warm ones.
- Use a variety of hue intensities to add interest. Dark colors and bright colors tend to dominate. A small amount of a dark fabric will have more impact than a large amount of a light fabric. Be sure there is enough contrast between fabrics to be used beside each other.
- If the fabrics selected look a little dull, add a touch of black, white, or yellow. To soften strong contrast, add a little gray.

Fabrics

QUILT TOP

One-hundred-percent cotton is traditionally the preferred fabric for quilting. Cotton has minimal distortion, holds pressing and creases well, is more durable than most other fabrics, and the needle glides through it more easily when hand quilting. There is an enormous selection of colors and prints available. Choose fabrics with a tight, even weave. Cotton-polyester blends fade less and wash and wear well, making them a good choice for children's quilts and projects that are handled often.

BACKING

Use the same weight fabric as the quilt top. Cotton prints are available up to 90" (229 cm) wide. Unbleached muslin is another popular choice.

BATTING

Bonded polyester is the most common batting, though needle-punched cotton and wool battings are available for quilters who prefer to use natural fibers. Use low-loft batting for hand and machine quilting, high loft for quilts that are to be tied. For machine stippling, cotton batting gives the best results. Choose dark-colored batting for deep-toned quilts, so if bearding (fibers migrating through the surface) occurs, it will not be too visible. Fusible fleece works well for smaller quilting projects.

BINDING

Join strips of bias-cut fabric to make your own, or purchase prepackaged quilt binding.

Making the Quilt Top

PREPARING FABRIC

Always prewash fabrics to remove sizing, test for colorfastness, and allow for any shrinkage. Don't use fabrics that continue to bleed after several rinsings. Press fabric before cutting to ensure greater accuracy. Square up fabric before you begin cutting. Pull on the bias grain and press. Trim selvages or avoid them to prevent seam puckering.

PATTERNS AND TEMPLATES

The patterns in this book are full size. Patchwork patterns include a $1/4$" (6 mm) seam allowance; appliqué patterns do not include seam allowance. To make a template, trace patterns onto tracing paper, then glue to cardboard and cut out, or trace directly onto template plastic and cut out. Label templates and mark grainlines and the number of each piece needed. Before marking directly onto fabric, test that the marker disappears or will not run when wet. Trace templates onto the wrong side of the fabric. Before cutting out the quilt top, make a sample block to test pattern accuracy.

CUTTING

Always cut and reserve any backing, sashing, bands, or borders before cutting small patches. Cut patches with sharp dressmaking shears or with a rotary cutter (see On the Cutting Edge, page 14).

PIECING

Pin patches together with right sides facing. Stitch them with a $1/4$" (6 mm) seam. Save time by "stringing" patches together: sew the first pair of patches; then, without lifting the presser foot, feed the next pair under the presser foot and so on. Clip the threads between the patches. Press all seams open at every piecing step. Piece patches, then piece patches together into bands, then bands into blocks, following individual project instructions. Stitch blocks together into rows, then rows together, adding sashing (bands of fabric) between rows if required. Stitch borders in place to complete the quilt top.

APPLIQUÉ

To provide stability to appliqué motifs, use a base, such as freezer paper, fusible web or interfacing, or a water-soluble stabilizer. If using freezer paper, cut it into the appliqué shape. Cut fabric $1/4$" (6 mm) larger. Place freezer paper on wrong side of fabric shape and press. The paper will adhere temporarily to the fabric. Follow manufacturer's instructions for using paper-backed fusibles or stabilizers. Fusibles will adhere an appliqué to the base fabric, without seam allowances to turn to the wrong side. Take care that none of the fusible touches the iron surface. A water-soluble stabilizer acts as a lining. Sew it to an appliqué shape, with right sides together. Snip an opening in the back and turn to the right side. The seam allowances are held in place by the stabilizer, which can be washed away after the quilt top is completed. Appliqués can be stitched in place with satin stitching (narrow, closely spaced zigzag) or with decorative stitches.

ON THE CUTTING EDGE

Quilting

TIPS FOR ROTARY CUTTING

- Press fabrics before cutting.
- Lay fabric on a self-healing cutting mat, keeping the grain parallel to the marked grid.
- Lay a ruler or straightedge on the fabric, to the left of the desired cutting line, with the majority of the fabric to the left (to the right if you're left-handed).
- Spread your hand out as wide as possible on the ruler and press down firmly. A ruler at least 6" (15 cm) wide is easier to hold.
- Place the rotary cutter against the ruler and push gently downward to cut through all layers. Hold the cutter upright, perpendicular to the fabric, never angled.
- Always cut by pushing the cutter away from your body, never toward you. Keep the hand holding the ruler behind the path of the cutter at all times. Apply as much pressure as necessary to cut through all layers.
- When cutting strips across the width of the fabric, fold fabric in half, then in half again. Stack several layers, place a ruler across them perpendicular to the fold, then cut across.
- For cutting patches, lay the template on a fabric stack, then place the ruler along the edge of the template and cut.
- Smaller cutters are easier to maneuver on curves.
- Keep blades for cutting fabric and paper separate. Mark blades with a permanent marker.
- Always remember to keep the blade retracted or the safety shield in place.
- Change blades often to minimize hand fatigue.

QUILTING DESIGNS

The most common quilting designs are outline quilting, echo quilting, in-the-ditch quilting, filler quilting, and motif quilting.

Outline quilting refers to quilting around a motif, usually 1/4" (6 mm) away, working just beyond the seam allowance.

Echo quilting refers to working continuous lines of quilting 1/4" (6 mm) beyond the first outline.

To quilt **in-the-ditch,** work stitches into the ridge or "ditch" of the seamline while gently pulling the seam apart. The stitches will disappear into the seamline.

Filler quilting refers to background designs that fill in the remaining areas of a quilt. These include stippling, grids, or straight lines.

There are many traditional **motifs** used for quilting. These are marked through a stencil or with tracing paper.

To mark quilting lines on a quilt top, press the quilt top, then secure it to a flat surface with masking tape. Begin marking from the center out to the borders with a disappearing marker, a lead pencil, or chalk.

BUILDING THE SANDWICH

Place the backing fabric on a flat surface (usually a clean floor) with the wrong side facing up. Tape it in place with masking tape. Fluff batting in a clothes dryer for several minutes to remove any wrinkles and center it on top of the backing. Baste a horizontal and vertical line through the two layers. Center the quilt top on the batting. Thread-baste the layers together, beginning at the center and working horizontally, vertically, and diagonally out to the edges. Baste the outer edges in place. Alternately, baste the layers together with safety pins, placing them through all three layers at regular intervals, no more than 6" (15 cm) apart.

HAND QUILTING

Thread a quilting needle with a 20" (51 cm) length of thread. Place the quilt in a hoop or frame. Knot one end of the thread. Begin quilting at the center and work out to the edges. Insert the needle into the quilt top and batting about 2" (5 cm) away from the beginning of the quilting line. Bring the needle out at the beginning point. Gently pull the thread to bury the knot inside the quilt sandwich. Make short running stitches through all three layers along marked quilting lines.

Place your free hand under the quilt to guide the needle back through the layers.

MACHINE QUILTING

Set machine for straight stitch—about 12 stitches per 1" (2.5 cm). Attach a walking foot or quilting foot to your machine. Roll half of the quilt tightly and secure with safety pins (bicycle clamps also work well). Slide the roll under the head of the sewing machine. Begin stitching at the center and work out to the edges. To change direction, lower the needle into the fabric, raise the

presser foot, pivot, then lower the presser foot. When stitching parallel designs, stitch in one direction to avoid puckering. To stitch small intricate areas, you may wish to use a hoop.

Finishing Your Quilt

When quilting is completed, the raw edges of the sandwich need to be bound together to finish the quilt. Trim the backing and batting even with the quilt top.

Press binding strips $1/4$" (6 mm) to the wrong side along one long edge, or use purchased binding. With right sides together, pin the raw unpressed edge of the binding strip to the edge of the quilt and stitch in place with a $1/4$" (6 mm) seam. For purchased binding, unfold one side of the binding and pin in place, matching the raw edges. Stitch in place along the foldline.

To miter corners, stitch borders to $1/4$" (6 mm) from each corner. Remove quilt from machine. Smooth one border over an adjacent one and draw a diagonal line from the inner seamline to the point where the outer edges cross. Reverse the borders and mark the other one in the same manner. With right sides together and top edges even, match the pencil lines and stitch through them.

Turn the binding to the back of the quilt and slip-stitch the folded edge in place by hand, or increase the amount of fabric folded to the back and machine-stitch in-the-ditch from the right side, catching the folded edge in the stitching.

Trim seam allowance to $1/4$" (6 mm). Turn the quilt over. Fold the stitched corner diagonally across the point of the quilt corner. Fold the binding along the foldline, with the corners meeting at the stitched line. Slipstitch the binding and miter in place.

Enjoying and Caring for Your Quilts

HANGING QUILTS

When making a quilt to hang for display, consider size and materials—overly large or heavy quilts will not hang well. Hang quilts in low traffic areas where they will not be touched. To avoid fading or damage to the fabric, keep them away from direct sunlight or bright spotlights, fireplaces, radiators, heat ducts, and stoves. Never pin, nail, tack, or glue a quilt to a wall. The best ways to hang a quilt are to make a rod pocket (see Making a Hanging Sleeve, below), to attach strips of VELCRO® or snap tape, or to purchase a quilt wall-hanging clamp. If using VELCRO®, attach the loop side to a muslin strip, then hand-sew the strip to the top of the quilt back. Attach the hook side to a strip of wood and then attach the wood to the wall; press the quilt in place. For snap tape, staple one side of the tape to a wood strip and attach to the wall. Hand-sew the other side of the tape to the back of the quilt, 1/2" (1.3 cm) from the top. Wall-hanging clamps, which are available in a variety of lengths, hold a quilt between two pieces of wood and do not require the attachment of extra fabric.

Clean hanging quilts with a vacuum cleaner. Hold a piece of window screen over the quilt to protect the fabric while the dirt is being removed with the vacuum.

CARE AND STORAGE

It is a quilter's axiom that the best place to store quilts is on the bed. Keep them away from sunlight to prevent fading and away from areas of high humidity and fluctuations in temperature to prevent damage to the fibers. Do not place quilts next to wood or cardboard as the chemicals found in them can discolor the fabrics.

Quilts should be cleaned thoroughly before storing. Wash them in a bathtub of lukewarm water with a mild soap. Air-dry completely. Fold loosely, pad the folds with acid-free tissue paper or washed, unbleached cotton to prevent sharp creases. If possible, roll quilts into a tube. Store in a cloth bag—make it from unbleached muslin or use cotton pillowcases—or in acid-free boxes, paper, or tubes. It's a good idea to refold quilts at least once a year to prevent permanent creasing.

MAKING A HANGING SLEEVE

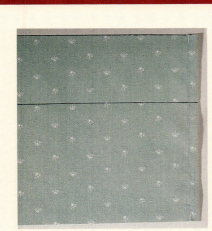

Cut a strip of fabric the width of the quilt by 8" (20.5 cm). Press the short ends 1/4" (6 mm) to the wrong side twice and stitch in place. With pencil, mark a line on right side 3" (7.5 cm) from one long edge.

With right sides together, fold the sleeve in half lengthwise. Stitch the long edges together with a 1/2" (1.3 cm) seam. Turn right side out and fold along the seam and press. Press along the marked pencil line.

Pin the pressed edges of the sleeve to the wrong side of the quilt top, forming a pocket. Slipstitch in place along both edges. Slip a strip of wood into the pocket and attach to hooks on the wall.

Amish Star Quilt

Bold and contemporary. This striking quilt has its roots in the traditional Ohio Star quilt block and the vivid colors favored by the Amish. Simple block construction techniques help demystify the piecing process.

SIZE

Quilt is 64" x 75" (163 cm x 191 cm)

MATERIALS

- 4 yds. (3.7 m) black broadcloth
- 2¼ yds. (2.1 m) backing fabric, 90" (229 cm) wide
- 1 yd. (1 m) black ikat fabric, 45" (115 cm) wide
- ⅛ yd. (.15 m) each of 15 assorted cotton print fabrics
- 9 yds. (8.25 m) gold double-fold bias binding
- Dark-colored quilt batting
- Sewing thread and black quilting thread
- Quilting needles
- Quilter's marking pencil
- Patchwork presser foot

CUTTING

Note: Prewash and press all fabrics. Patterns on page 120 include ¼" (6 mm) seam allowance.

Black broadcloth

Cut 2 strips each 2½" x 57½" (6.5 cm x 146 cm) and 2 strips each 2½" x 64½" (6.5 cm x 164 cm) for inner borders.

Cut 24 strips each 2½" x 9½" (6.5 cm x 24 cm) and 5 strips each 2½" x 53½" (6.5 cm x 136 cm) for sashing.

Cut 120 pieces each of pattern A squares and pattern B triangles (page 120).

Ikat

Cut 4 strips each 3½" x 32¼" (9 cm x 82 cm) and 3½" x 34¾" (9 cm x 88 cm) for outer borders.

Print fabrics

From each of 15 prints, cut 2 pattern A square pieces and 24 pattern B triangle pieces.

Stitch black A squares to both sides of 2 pieced squares to make top and bottom rows of star block. Join remaining pieced squares to either side of print A square to make center row.

Join rows to make star block. Make 30 blocks in same manner.

PIECING

Using patchwork foot, join 4 black B pieces to 4 print B pieces to form larger triangles. Likewise join 4 pairs of print B pieces.

Join pairs of pieced print and print/black triangles together to make squares.

ASSEMBLY

Following Quilt Assembly Diagram on page 20, join blocks into 6 rows of 5 blocks each with short sashing strips between each block; join rows with long sashing strips. Stitch long black inner border strips to sides and short black inner border strips to top and bottom of quilt top. Join pairs of ikat strips along shorter ends to make 2 borders each 63½" (161 cm) and 68½" (174 cm) long. Stitch outer borders in place in same manner as inner borders.

HAND QUILTING

With quilter's marking pencil, mark border quilting pattern (blue lines on Assembly Diagram) on quilt top. Lay backing fabric wrong side up on work surface. Center batting on backing, then place quilt top, right side up, on top. Beginning at center, baste layers together. With quilting thread, hand-quilt 1/4" (6 mm) outside each pieced star and along marked lines through all layers.

Quilt Assembly Diagram

FINISHING

Trim batting and backing even with quilt top. Machine-stitch binding to right side of quilt.

Fold binding to wrong side of quilt and slipstitch in place. Whipstitch ends together.

Harvest Stars Wall Hanging

Prairie Point edging was a favorite finishing with quilters of the Old West. The distinctive border echoed the quilt's colors and made use of leftover block scraps. The combination of machine-quilting techniques on this quilt gives the stars rich dimension.

SIZE

Wall hanging is 38" (96.5 cm) square. With Prairie Points it is 41" (104 cm) square.

MATERIALS

- 2 1/2 yds. (2.3 m) cream cotton print fabric
- 1/2 yd. (.5 m) medium green cotton print fabric
- 1/4 yd. (.25 m) each of 3 pairs of assorted light and medium tone cotton print fabrics, and light green
- Low-loft cotton quilt batting
- Cream sewing and quilting threads
- Safety pins
- Precut quilt border stencil, 2" (5 cm) maximum width
- Quilter's marking pencil
- Patchwork foot, walking foot, and machine-quilting presser foot

CUTTING

Note: Prewash and press all fabrics. Patterns on page 120 include 1/4" (6 mm) seam allowance.

Cream

Cut a 40" (101.5 cm) square piece for backing.

Cut 2 strips each 3 1/2" x 33 1/2" (9 cm x 85 cm) and 2 strips each 3 1/2" x 38 1/2" (9 cm x 98 cm) for inner borders.

Cut 2 strips each 2 1/2" x 31 1/2" (6.5 cm x 80 cm) and 6 strips each 2 1/2" x 9 1/2" (6.5 cm x 24 cm) for sashing.

Cut 36 pieces each of pattern A square and pattern B triangle (page 120).

Cut 8" x 39" (20.5 cm x 99.5 cm) strip for hanging sleeve.

Print fabrics

From medium green, cut 2 strips each 1 1/2" x 31 1/2" (3.8 cm x 80 cm) and 2 strips each 1 1/2" x 33 1/2" (3.8 cm x 85 cm) for inner borders.

From each assorted print, cut 1 A square and 12 B triangles.

From light green, cut 2 A squares and 16 B triangles; from medium green, cut 1 A square and 20 B triangles.

Cut 8 A squares of each print for border points.

PRAIRIE POINTS

Press border point squares in half diagonally, then in half diagonally once again.

Beginning at one corner and with raw edges matching, pin points evenly around quilt top, placing one triangle inside fold of previous triangle. Stitch points in place, 1/4" (6 mm) from raw edges.

PIECING

Using patchwork presser foot, join 4 cream B pieces to 4 medium print B pieces to form larger triangles. Join 4 light print B pieces to 4 medium print B pieces in same manner. Join pairs of pieced cream/medium print and light print/medium print triangles together to make squares. Stitch cream A squares to both sides of 2 pieced squares to make top and bottom rows of star block. Join remaining pieced squares to either side of print A square to make center row. Join rows to make star block. Make 9 blocks, reversing the medium print and light print position for 4 of the blocks.

ASSEMBLY

Following Wall Hanging Assembly Diagram, join blocks into 3 rows of 3 blocks each with short sashing strips between each block; join rows with long sashing strips. Stitch shorter green border strips to top and bottom and longer green border strips to sides of quilt top. Stitch cream border strips in place in same manner.

MACHINE QUILTING

With quilter's marking pencil and quilting stencil, center and mark border quilting pattern inside cream outer border. Lay backing fabric wrong side up on work surface. Center batting on backing, then place quilt top, right side up, on top. Beginning at center, pin layers together with safety pins. To machine-quilt, set machine for straight stitching.

With walking foot, machine-quilt *in-the-ditch* around stars and each center square. To stitch in-the-ditch, spread fabric apart at seamlines and stitch along the seam. Release fabric and stitches will disappear into seamlines.

With patchwork foot, *echo-quilt* around star motifs, repeating the shape of the stars. Work a row of quilting 1/4" (6 mm) from the stars, then 1/4" (6 mm) away again, with points meeting at the center of each sashing strip.

Stipple-quilt to fill the remaining cream background inside the outer green borders. With quilting presser foot and feed dogs lowered, work random stitching, keeping stitching lines close together and density consistent. Practice on scrap fabric before beginning.

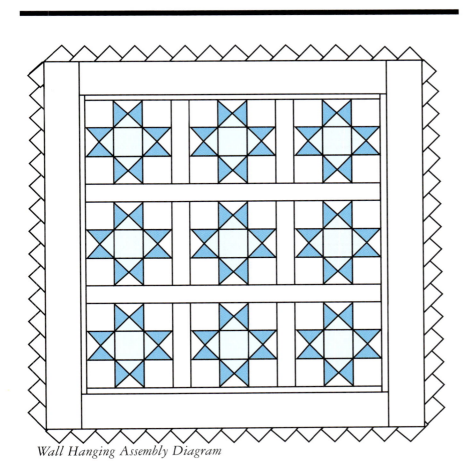

Wall Hanging Assembly Diagram

With walking foot, machine-quilt along marked border lines.

FINISHING

Trim batting even with quilt top. Trim backing 1/2" (1.3 cm) larger than quilt top. Press backing 1/2" (1.3 cm) to wrong side and fold over raw edge of batting so that folded edge covers Prairie Point stitching line. Pin all layers in place. Machine-stitch layers in place on quilt front 1/8" (3 mm) from Prairie Points. To make hanging sleeve, see page 17.

Log Cabin Pillows

A symbol of our heritage, the Log Cabin is one of the most popular patchwork motifs. Its graphic appeal comes from contrasting light and dark strips set in a variety of patterns. Folded strips stitched in layers around a center square are a unique variation on the classic technique.

SIZE

Pillows are 14" (35.5 cm) square

MATERIALS

Note: Materials and instructions are for a set of 3 pillows.

- 3 yds. (2.75 m) black broadcloth
- 1 yd. (1 m) dark blue cotton print fabric
- 1 yd. (1 m) lightweight muslin
- 1/2 yd. (.5 m) jade cotton print fabric
- 1/4 yd. (.25 m) each of fuchsia and purple cotton print fabrics
- Small amounts of mustard, pink, and wine cotton print fabrics
- Pencil and ruler
- Rotary cutter and cutting mat
- Black sewing thread
- Small amount of fusible web
- Polyester fiberfill

CUTTING

Note: Prewash and press all fabrics. Pillows include 1/2" (1.3 cm) seam allowance.

Pillow backs

From black, cut 3 pillow backs each 15" (38 cm) square.

Blocks

From mustard, cut 9 squares each 2" (5 cm) for centers. Cut fusible web same size for each square.

Across fabric width with rotary cutter as needed, cut remaining print fabrics and black broadcloth into strips 2" (5 cm) wide.

Across fabric width with rotary cutter for Pillows 1 and 2, cut 4 dark blue border strips 1 1/2" (3.8 cm) wide.

Bases

From muslin, cut an 18" (46 cm) square block and 8 square blocks each 10" (25 cm).

MARKING THE BASE

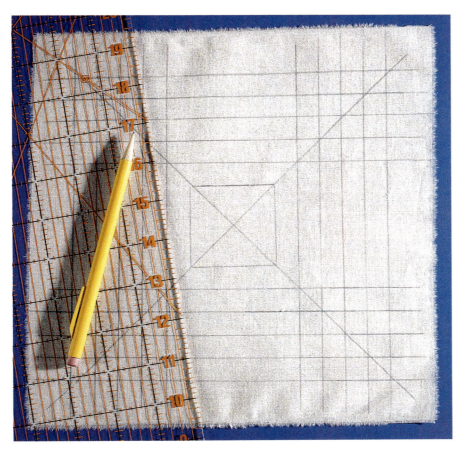

With pencil and ruler, mark diagonal lines onto muslin bases, joining opposite corners. At centers, where lines cross, draw a 2" (5 cm) square. Mark lines around each side of center squares 1/2" (1.3 cm) apart. Mark 5 rows on small blocks, 12 rows on large block.

STITCHING STRIPS

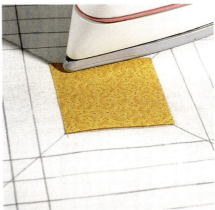

Following manufacturer's instructions for using fusible web, fuse mustard center square right side up on muslin base.

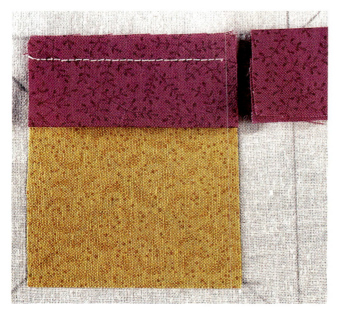

Press all strips except dark blue border strips in half lengthwise with wrong sides together. Beginning with a pink strip, line up one end with the edge of the center square, matching raw edges with the first marked line. Pin the strip in place. Stitch 1/4" (6 mm) from the raw edge, ending at next corner of center square. Trim the strip even with the center square.

Continue turning in the same direction and stitching strips in place. Stitch colored strips in the order listed for each pillow (see Variations, below). For small blocks, stitch 5 rows of strips, for large block, 12 rows. Secure strip ends on outermost round.

VARIATIONS

Pillows are numbered as they appear left to right on page 24.

Pillow 1: Stitch strips in following order: pink, wine, purple, jade, and blue. Stitch 4 blocks together with blue sides matching at center. With right sides together, stitch dark blue border strips to top and bottom edges of 4-block square. Trim and press open. Stitch strips to remaining sides.

Pillow 2: Stitch strips in following order: pink, fuchsia, purple, jade, and blue. Stitch 4 blocks together with blue corners of 2 diagonally opposite blocks and black corners from remaining blocks meeting at center. With right sides together, stitch dark blue border strips to top and bottom edges of 4-block square. Trim and press open. Stitch strips to remaining sides.

Pillow 3: Stitch strips in following order: pink, 2 rows fuchsia, 3 rows each of purple, jade, and blue.

Turn the muslin counterclockwise. Place a pink strip along this side, overlapping and matching the end with the first strip and the raw edges with the marked line. Stitch in place and trim the strip as before. Turn and stitch black strips to the remaining two sides.

FINISHING

Trim muslin even with last strip. Stitch pillow backs to fronts, leaving an opening for turning. Turn right side out and press. Lightly stuff pillow with fiberfill and slipstitch opening closed.

Crazy-Quilt Christmas Stockings

Opulent fabrics and elegant embellishments are the hallmarks of Victorian crazy quilting. The tradition continues with these heirloom stockings, updated with fast machine piecing and hi-tech embroidery that's worked on luxurious jewel tones and sophisticated ivories and creams.

SIZE

Stockings are 16" (43 cm) tall

MATERIALS

Note: Materials and instructions are for one stocking only.

- ½ yd. (.5 m) each of dark green moiré and dark rose velvet **or** ivory moiré and ivory velvet
- 15" x 22" (38 cm x 56 cm) piece lightweight muslin
- Remnants of assorted satin, velvet, and taffeta fabrics in roses and greens **or** linens, dotted Swiss, and cotton fabrics in ivories, creams, and light pinks
- Small amount of cream embossed satin **or** cream lace for cuff
- Assorted remnants of cream laces and trims
- Assorted charms, beads, buttons, and pearls
- 1 yd. (1 m) each of green, rose, and metallic gold ribbons **or** 3 yds. (2.75 m) of 1" (2.5 cm) wide cream silk ribbon and 1 yd. (1 m) each of pink and green narrow silk ribbons and gold metallic ribbon ¾" (2 cm) wide
- Matching sewing threads
- Metallic or rayon machine embroidery threads
- Machine embroidery foot
- Twin needle and pin tuck foot for ivory stocking

CUTTING

Note: Stocking pattern on page 120 includes ¼" (6 mm) seam allowance.

Stocking

From velvet, cut 1 stocking back.

From moiré, cut 1 pair of stocking linings.

From cream satin, cut a 3½" x 9" (9 cm x 23 cm) cuff.

Cut assorted remnant fabrics into small rectangular patch pieces and one 5-sided piece for rose stocking.

CRAZY QUILTING

Mark stocking outline onto muslin. Mark heel. For rose stocking, place 5-sided patch in center of stocking and pin in place. For ivory stocking, work rows of pin tucks on a larger piece of fabric, then perpendicular rows across the first set as desired. Center on stocking and pin in place.

Place a second patch over the first, right sides together, matching any raw edge. Stitch ¼" (6 mm) from edge, for the length of the first patch.

Trim remaining patch fabric as shown. Press patch to right side and pin opposite edge in place.

Continue adding patches in the same manner, working around the first patch in one direction until all sides of center patch are covered. For heel, work patches in a sunburst radiating from the heel, and trim them even with marked heel line. Add patches until outline of stocking is filled.

MACHINE EMBROIDERY

Thread machine with embroidery thread, bobbin with cotton thread. Following manufacturer's instructions, set machine for decorative embroidery stitching. Stitch motifs and rows of decorative stitches inside patches as desired.

FINISHING

Cut out pieced stocking same size as backing. Fold cuff in half lengthwise and match raw edges with top and sides of stocking front. Baste raw edges in place. Stitch stocking front to back with 1/4" (6 mm) seam. Turn right side out. Stitch linings together, leaving a 3" (7.5 cm) opening at the center of one side.

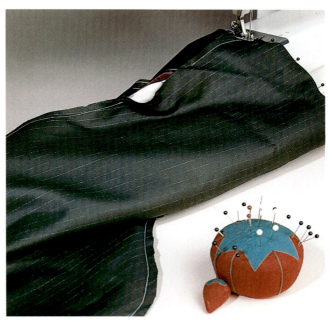

With right sides together, slip stocking inside lining. Match upper raw edges and side seams; pin in place. Stitch upper edges of stocking and lining together. Turn stocking right side out through opening in lining. Slipstitch opening closed. Push lining into stocking and press edges to hold in place.

Using photo on page 27 for inspiration, embellish stocking as desired, hand-sewing elements in place. For rose stocking, cut ribbons in half. Holding ribbons together, tie into a bow and sew to upper edge of stocking. For ivory stocking, gather 18" (46 cm) lengths of wide silk ribbon to make roses. Sew 3 roses and metallic bows to cuff, and stitch a cream ribbon hanger in place.

TIP

When sewing with metallic embroidery threads, apply several drops of needle lubricant to the needle, following manufacturer's instructions. It will glide through the fabric more easily.

Noah's Ark Crib Quilt

Bring a biblical classic to life for a child you love. A collection of muted plaids forms an unusual backdrop for easy appliqué and machine blanket stitching, which adds to the appealing folk-art quality of this cozy picture-quilt.

SIZE

Quilt is 34" x 46½" (86.5 cm x 118 cm)

MATERIALS

- 1⅜ yd. (1.30 m) cotton print backing fabric
- ½ yd. (.5 m) gray gingham for binding
- ½ yd. (.5 m) pink plaid for ark
- ⅜ yd. (.35 m) each of 2 plaids for sky and ocean bands
- ¼ yd. (.25 m) each of 2 plaids for wave and ocean floor bands and 2 plaids for pieced borders
- Remnants of 13 assorted plaid and striped cotton fabrics for appliqués
- Water-soluble stabilizer
- Low-loft quilt batting
- Sewing threads in white and dark blue
- Safety pins
- Quilter's marking pencil
- Embroidery foot and walking foot

CUTTING

Note: Prewash and press all fabrics. Patterns on pages 121-123 **do not** include seam allowance.

Bands

Cut an 11" x 33½" (28 cm x 85 cm) piece for sky (band A).
Cut a 6½" x 33½" (16.5 cm x 85 cm) piece for ocean (band B).
Cut an 8" x 33½" (20.5 cm x 85 cm) piece for waves (band C).
Cut a 9¼" x 33½" (23.5 cm x 85 cm) piece for ocean floor (band D).
From remnants, cut 4 assorted blocks each 8½" x 9½" (21.5 cm x 24 cm) for topmost band.

Borders

Cut 4 strips 2" x 44" (5 cm x 112 cm) from each of 2 border fabrics.

Backing

Cut a 34" x 47" (86.5 cm x 119.5 cm) piece.

Binding

Cut and piece 2" (5 cm) wide strips to make a 165" (429 cm) long binding strip.

APPLIQUÉ

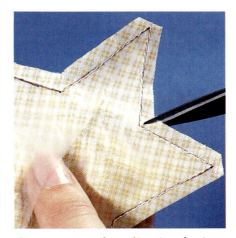

Trace outlines of appliqué patterns (pages 121-123) to stabilizer. For ark, fold stabilizer in half to mark vertical center. Place half pattern against fold and trace. Flip stabilizer and trace reverse on other side. Trace waves across upper edge of a band of stabilizer 8" (20.5 cm) wide (band C).

Cut out tracings, leaving extra fabric around the edges, and place stabilizer on back of fabric with right sides together. With machine set at short stitch length, stitch fabric and stabilizer together along marked lines.

Cut out around appliqué and trim seam allowances to ⅛" (3 mm), then clip all curves and points.

Pull stabilizer away from fabric and cut a slit across center back of stabilizer within appliqué shape. Turn right side out. Press appliqué flat on right side. Do not allow iron to make contact with stabilizer.

Following photo (page 30) and assembly diagram, stitch bands A and B together. Pin ark and giraffe appliqués in place. With embroidery foot and blue thread, set machine for blanket stitch. Stitch outer edges of ark in place with straight stitches on base fabric and perpendicular stitches falling onto appliqué, and stitching over lower edge of giraffe.

In same manner, stitch giraffe in place; stitch cat to inner window square and place inside ark window; stitch inner edge of window in place. Matching lower raw edges, stitch upper edge of waves to band B and ark. Stitch band D below waves. Stitch fish and turtle in place. Stitch animal appliqués to center of each of 4 remnant blocks. Following manufacturer's instructions, wash quilt top to remove stabilizer. Press.

ASSEMBLY

Stitch animal blocks together to make topmost band. Stitch band to top of quilt top. With right sides together, stitch each pair of border strips together along one long edge with a 1/4" (6 mm) seam. Cut pieced borders at 2" (5 cm) intervals to make 44 pieced squares. Stitch pieced squares together, alternating direction of colored squares, to make 2 borders each with 22 pairs of squares. Stitch borders in place to top and bottom of quilt top.

MACHINE QUILTING

With quilter's marking pencil, mark quilting patterns (blue lines on Assembly Diagram, page 33) onto quilt top. Lay backing fabric wrong side up on work surface. Center batting on backing, then place quilt top, right side up, on top. Beginning at center, pin layers together with safety pins. To machine-quilt, set machine for straight stitching and attach walking foot. Quilt along marked lines. Quilt 1/4" (6 mm) inside edge of ark and around window.

FINISHING

Trim batting and backing even with quilt top. Press one long edge of binding strip 1/2" (1.3 cm) to wrong side twice. With right sides together, pin unpressed edges of binding strip to front of quilt. Stitch in place with a 3/8" (1 cm) seam. Turn pressed edges to wrong side and pin in place. Stitch binding in place through all layers by stitching in-the-ditch.

Band
A

Band
B

Band
C

Band
D

Crib Quilt Assembly Diagram

CHAPTER 2

Creating Cherished Heirlooms

Sewing heirloom pieces allows you to create fantasies with beautiful laces, exquisite trims, and lush fabrics, all worked with the delicacy of detail saved for special projects. The love and care put into making a one-of-a-kind gift or memento for a special occasion can be seen in every stitch. Both the giver and the receiver are enriched and touched by the results of this very personal creative endeavor. The elegant, detailed handwork of yesterday, which included decorative sewing techniques, such as pin tucking and embroidery, worked on fine fabrics, can be duplicated with the use of today's sewing technology.

The Basics

Making heirlooms to pass along in your family or to give as gifts to celebrate special occasions is one of the true joys of sewing. Before you begin, read this section, which offers information and tips for working with fabrics and materials that deserve special handling and attention.

Tools of the Trade

Heirloom sewing requires tools and supplies for working with materials that are more delicate than those used for basic sewing. The following guidelines will help you select the materials you'll need to make the projects in this chapter.

CUTTING

Sharp dressmaking shears. They should be at least 8" (20.5 cm) long with comfortable handles.

Small, sharp-pointed embroidery scissors. These are necessary for cutting lace and fine fabric, and detailed designs.

Appliqué scissors. The flange holds lace at a safe distance from the blade when cutting away a fabric layer.

Paper scissors. Use these for cutting patterns and stabilizers, so as not to blunt shears that are used for cutting fabric.

MARKING

Disappearing markers. Pens or pencils that are either water-soluble or will gradually fade over a short period of time. Test first on scrap fabric before using them to trace designs for cutwork or guidelines for pin tucks or machine embroidery.

Iron-on transfer pens. These are ideal for opaque fabrics, but designs must be reversed. They are usually water-soluble on cotton.

Test them on your fabric before beginning.

Dressmaker's carbon or transfer paper. Follow manufacturer's instructions for use.

NEEDLES AND PINS

Silk pins. Finer than regular pins, these are less likely to mark delicate fabrics.

Sewing needles. Choose fine needles, such as sharps or betweens, with a small eye and even thickness for hand sewing.

Machine needles. Use fine needles, size 70/10, that are compatible with the fabric and thread being used for your project. Consult your machine manual.

Double or twin needles. Two needles attached to the same shank, used for making machine pin tucks. They are available in a variety of widths and are designed to work with specific presser feet.

THREADS

Match the thread content to the fiber content of the fabric whenever possible. Use fine 100 percent cotton, rayon, or silk. For decorative stitching and embroidery, use a heavier weight rayon, metallic, or other decorative thread that has a lustrous sheen. Contrasting colors will highlight stitch details.

STABILIZERS

When working with fine fabrics, add a backing so that fabric will feed evenly and not bunch when decorative-stitching or embroidering. Use tissue paper, freezer paper, or purchased wash-away, tear-away, iron-away, or liquid stabilizers. Follow manufacturer's instructions for the best results.

GLUES AND FUSIBLES

Never use these on heirloom projects that are to be laundered or have any use other than a decorative one. When gluing, use a water-based white craft glue. Fusible web backed with a release paper can be used for making fabric or a motif into an iron-on; this is particularly useful for covering bandboxes. When applying ribbons and trims to decorator pieces, use fusible tape.

MACHINE SEWING

A sewing machine with a zigzag stitch is essential for heirloom sewing techniques, such as joining laces and trims to each other and to fabric. Other stitch features that will be helpful include satin stitch, decorative stitches and preprogrammed embroidery stitches, such as flowers, leaves, and bows. A machine that accommodates a twin needle for pin tucking and various presser feet (see Performing Feet, below) will increase your creativity. A machine embroidery hoop will maintain fabric tautness when machine embroidering.

PERFORMING FEET

Creating interesting stitch details, embroidering, and applying laces and trims require the use of specialized presser feet. If you don't already have them, they are worth the investment to ensure successful results for your fine sewing.

PIN TUCK FEET are available in a variety of sizes to suit the weight of fabric being worked on and the desired size of the finished pin tucks. The grooves on the bottom of the feet keep the pin tucks aligned; fewer grooves make larger, widely spaced tucks.

Left to right:
GATHERING FOOT will create tight, even gathers, and will gather one layer while stitching it to another.
EDGESTITCH FOOT is used to attach lace and ribbon to fabric and for sewing decorative edges.
EMBROIDERY FOOT has a wide, open toe for increased visibility and for smoother feeding over satin stitching.

LACES AND TRIMS

Heirloom projects are enhanced by the addition of exquisite laces, beautiful ribbons, and elegant trims. Use cotton laces with natural fabrics. This list will help you select the most appropriate trim for your project.

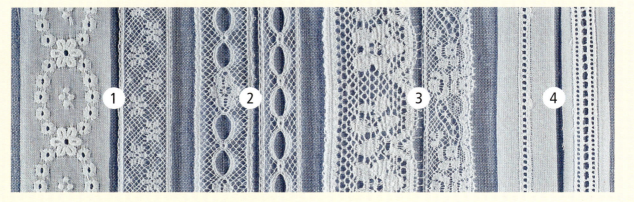

1. INSERTION LACE has two straight edges for joining between two pieces of fabric. It comes in many varieties.
2. BEADING LACE has evenly spaced openings for threading narrow ribbon.
3. EDGING LACE has one straight edge for stitching to fabric and a decorative scalloped edge. It is available in a variety of widths.
4. ENTREDEUX is an embroidery trim placed between two laces or fabrics to join them with a row of decorative openwork. It is a strip of small, evenly spaced holes.

Not shown:
LACE MOTIFS AND MEDALLIONS are available in a variety of sizes, shapes, and designs for embellishing.
DECORATIVE RIBBONS in either silk or satin, with woven or wire edges, add color and dimension to projects.

Fabrics

CHOOSING FABRICS

One-hundred-percent natural, lightweight fabrics should be used for heirloom sewing. Traditionally heirlooms are sewn in white, cream or pastels. To create decorative pieces, choose silks, moirés, taffetas, linens, and other decorator fabrics.

Batiste. This is a cotton fabric available in three weights: very fine, fine, and medium. This is the preferred fabric for stitching clothing, christening dresses, and other heirloom pieces.

Linen. There are two weights generally used for heirloom sewing: cambric, a fine, glazed linen, is used for table linens; handkerchief linen is even finer and is popular for all types of heirloom sewing. Linen launders very well.

Organdy. A stiff, transparent cotton with a matte finish.

Organza. This is another stiff, transparent fabric, woven from silk and with a slight sheen.

Lawn. A fine, firm cotton fabric.

Silk. An extremely fine yet strong fabric, silk is available in a range of weights and has excellent draping qualities. It requires very careful laundering.

PREPARING FABRICS AND TRIMS

If necessary, wash fabrics to preshrink them, then iron while still damp. Lightly starch fabrics and trims to make them easier to work with. Draw out a thread across the ends of fabric and cut along the line formed to straighten fabric edges. If the grain is not straight, pull on the bias grain and iron to set it in place.

Patterns

Patterns in this book are full size, and include a 1/4" (6 mm) seam allowance. Trace them onto tracing paper and cut out. Label pattern pieces and mark grainlines where necessary.

Caring for Your Heirlooms

Handwash heirloom garments or linens in warm water with a mild, pure soap. Hang them to dry or dry flat rather than machine dry. Starch and iron with a pressing cloth. Store heirloom pieces folded flat in acid-free tissue paper.

Sewing Heirlooms

Sewing heirlooms utilizes specialized stitches and embroidery details. Follow these instructions for seams and stitching embellishments.

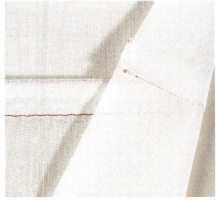

FRENCH SEAM

This neat, narrow seam encloses raw fabric edges. For seams with a 1/2" (1.3 cm) seam allowance, with wrong sides together and matching raw edges, stitch 1/4" (6 mm) from the edge. Carefully trim the seam to 1/8" (3 mm). Press the seam open, then with right sides together, crease along the seam; press. Stitch 1/4" (6 mm) from the fold, enclosing the raw edges.

OVERCAST EDGE SEAM

Use this seam on sheer fabrics when a regular width seam allowance would be distracting. With right sides together and matching raw edges, stitch along the seamline, then 1/8" (3 mm) away. Carefully trim the seam allowance close to the second row of stitching. Stitch a narrow zigzag over the second row of stitching, encasing the raw edges.

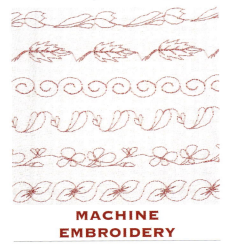

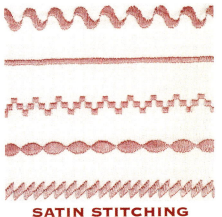

MACHINE EMBROIDERY

With an embroidery foot and using decorative threads if desired, set your machine for decorative stitching, referring to your machine manual for specific instructions. Use a stabilizer beneath fabric to prevent puckering, and an embroidery hoop if desired.

SATIN STITCHING

This is worked with an embroidery foot and your machine set for a closely spaced zigzag stitch (short stitch length). Adjust the stitch width as necessary for the design. Refer to your machine manual for specific instructions for decorative stitches composed of satin stitching.

PERFECT PIN TUCKS

Pin tucks are created with a pin-tuck presser foot, a twin needle, and two spools of thread. The twin needle makes two rows of stitches, with the bobbin thread pulling underneath to create a narrow ridge. The size of the foot will be determined by the weight of the fabric and the desired distance between the pin tucks. Consult your machine manual for needle and presser foot size.

1. Fold fabric in half along the grainline and press. You can determine the grainline by drawing a thread from the fabric.

2. Set up your machine with a presser foot, twin needle, and two spools of matching thread. To avoid tangling, take one thread to either side of the tension gauge and leave one thread out of the last thread guide before the needle.

3. Start the first row of stitching on the center fold.

4. To stitch a second row, place a presser foot groove on the first pin tuck and stitch another one. The first tuck will move through the groove in the foot, keeping the second pin tuck aligned. Always stitch pin tucks in the same direction.

5. To make corded pin tucks, thread cording or gimp through the hole in the needle plate. It will feed into the underside of the pin tuck between the two rows of stitching.

Sweetheart Pillow

A fancy cutaway lace bow highlights this charming boudoir pillow. Ruffles and lace, ribbons and beads, and decorative pin tucking add the embellishing touches to a labor of love for someone very special.

SIZE

Pillow is 10" x 10" (25 cm x 25 cm), plus ruffle

MATERIALS

- ■ 3/4 yd. (.75 m) cream dress-weight Swiss batiste
- ■ 12" (30.5 cm) square of pink batiste for lining
- ■ 1 yd. (1 m) cream insertion lace 2 3/4" (70 mm) wide
- ■ 3 yds. (2.75 m) pink ruffled ribbon 3/4" (20 mm) wide
- ■ 1 1/4 yds. (1.15 m) pregathered cream lace 1" (25 mm) wide
- ■ 1 yd. (1 m) pink satin ribbon 3/8" (10 mm) wide
- ■ Cream cotton thread
- ■ Pink rayon or cotton machine embroidery thread
- ■ Cream cordonnet thread
- ■ Tear-away stabilizer
- ■ Spray starch
- ■ 5 pink or pearl beads
- ■ Fiberfill
- ■ Tracing paper
- ■ 2.0/80 double needle
- ■ 7-groove pin tuck foot, embroidery foot, and edgestitch foot
- ■ Sharp-pointed embroidery or appliqué scissors

CUTTING

Cream Batiste

Cut 2 squares each 12" (30.5 cm).
Cut 2 ruffle strips each 6" x 45" (15 cm x 115 cm).

Stabilizer

Cut a 12" (30.5 cm) square.

CORDED PIN TUCKS

Draw a thread along the vertical center of one cream square to mark for the first pin tuck. Following machine manual, insert double needle, attach pin-tuck presser foot and set machine for straight stitch. Thread cordonnet up through the hole in the needle plate. Stitch a pin tuck along the line formed by the pulled thread, stitching over the cordonnet. Stitch 5 more pin tucks on either side of the center pin tuck, with each tuck 2 presser foot grooves apart.

LACE APPLIQUÉ

To make lace fabric, cut insertion lace into 3 equal lengths, long enough to cover the bow design. Lightly starch lace. With edge-stitch foot and a narrow zigzag, stitch the 3 pieces together to make lace fabric that will cover the bow.

Trace the appliqué bow pattern (page 124) onto the center of the tear-away stabilizer. Mark shaded areas that are to be cut away.

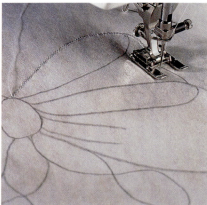

Lay pin-tucked batiste square wrong side up on work surface. Center lace fabric, wrong side up, on batiste, then place tear-away stabilizer, with marked design facing up, on top to make a sandwich. Pin sandwich layers together. With cotton thread and embroidery foot, stitch a narrow zigzag along the marked design lines. Remove from machine and turn sandwich over so that the batiste is on top.

With appliqué scissors, carefully trim batiste away from marked areas within the design, leaving lace and stabilizer layers intact. Thread machine with pink thread. Satin-stitch the bow design onto the batiste, covering the previous-

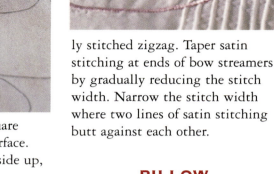

ly stitched zigzag. Taper satin stitching at ends of bow streamers by gradually reducing the stitch width. Narrow the stitch width where two lines of satin stitching butt against each other.

PILLOW

Following manufacturer's instructions, carefully remove stabilizer from the wrong side of the sandwich and trim away excess lace from edges of bow. Trace heart half-pattern (page 124) onto one half of tracing paper. Fold paper in half along dash line and cut out to make complete heart pattern. Center pattern over bow appliqué, matching top of bow to dot, and cut out. Cut heart from pink for lining and from cream for pillow back.

Stitch short edges of ruffle strips together to make a large loop. Press ruffle strip in half lengthwise. Stitch pink ruffled ribbon along the folded edge of the ruffle strip. Along raw edges of ruffle strip, make 2 rows of gathering stitches (straight stitch with a long stitch length) $1/8"$ (3 mm) apart. Pull up threads to gather ruffle to fit outer edge of heart. Matching gathered edges, baste pregathered lace to front of ruffle. Right sides together and matching raw edges, pin ruffle in place on heart front. Baste.

Lay pink lining fabric right side up on work surface. Place bow panel on top, right side up, to make pillow top. With right sides together, pin back to pillow top. Stitch together with a $1/2"$ (1.3 cm) seam, leaving an opening for turning along one side. Turn right side out, press. Stuff with fiberfill and slipstitch opening closed.

FINISHING

Tie satin ribbon into a bow and stitch to pillow front. Thread beads onto bow streamers and hand-sew to pillow.

TIPS

• Choose wide cotton lace with an all-over pattern and straight edges.
• To find the right side of your lace, look for the more textured side, it usually has raised or corded ridge outlines.
• Always stitch with thread the same color as the lace.
• Use a medium stitch length to zigzag two laces together; a tight stitch (short stitch length) will cause puckering.
• To stitch smooth curves, take the time to raise the presser foot and pivot your work often during the zigzag step.
• Test your satin stitch before beginning to see that it covers the zigzag stitch completely.
• To begin and end satin stitching, set stitch width at 0 and sew several stitches to secure. Pull thread ends to the wrong side and secure.
• To trim away fabric from behind an appliqué, use scissors with a flange to separate layers or with blunt ends to avoid catching the lace fibers.

Classic Cutwork

Re-create the elegance of nineteenth-century embroidered table linens with the time-honored technique of cutwork. Try your hand at a sophisticated table topper, napkin and ring, or a lovely lingerie bag.

SIZE

Cutwork pieces are 16" (40.5 cm) square

MATERIALS

Note: Materials and instructions are for one cutwork square.

- ½ yd. (.5 m) cambric or handkerchief linen in cream or blue
- 2 spools silk thread in light blue, light blue-green, or white
- 1 yd. (1 m) water-soluble stabilizer
- 2 pieces muslin each 20" (51 cm) square
- Water-soluble marking pen
- Spray starch
- 7" (18 cm) spring tension embroidery hoop
- Sharp-pointed embroidery or appliqué scissors
- Embroidery foot
- Purchased napkin ring (optional)

CUTTING

Linen
Cut an 18" (46 cm) square.
For napkin ring, cut a 6" (15 cm) square.

Stabilizer
Cut 4 squares each 18" (46 cm).
For napkin ring, cut 5 squares each 10" (25 cm).

PREPARATION

Press and lightly starch linen, straightening the grain of the fabric if necessary. Following manufacturer's instructions, fuse layers of stabilizer together between layers of muslin, taking care not to let water or iron touch stabilizer.

TRANSFERRING DESIGNS

Note: Tablemat has cutwork design worked on 4 corners; napkin and bag on 1 corner only.

With water-soluble marking pen, mark a square 1" (2.5 cm) in from edges of linen. Fold fabric square diagonally, press lightly, unfold and mark diagonal corner lines. Trace or photocopy same size corner design (page 126). Matching marked diagonals, transfer design to corner of linen with marker. Mark all four corners if desired. Mark the center of each side. Beginning at center and working to corners, trace scallops along each side.

BORDERS

Thread machine and bobbin with silk thread and attach embroidery foot. Place fused layers of stabilizer underneath linen and pin in place. With 1.5 stitch length, sew short straight stitches along marked scalloped border through all layers. At pivot points, lower needle into fabric, raise presser foot, pivot fabric, and replace presser foot before continuing. If your machine has preset scallop stitch capability, use it to straight-stitch the scallop borders along the marked border line.

With a narrow zigzag at a stitch length of 1.5 and width of 2, padstitch over the straight stitching. The needle should fall just clear of the straight stitching on the outer swing and fall into the body of the cutwork on the opposite swing.

Carefully trim away linen close to zigzag stitching, leaving layers of stabilizer intact.

Satin-stitch over the zigzag, with a stitch length of .3 to .5 and stitch width of 3, just clearing the edge of the fabric and stitching into the stabilizer.

CORNER MOTIF

Load the layers of linen and stabilizer with corner motif into spring tension hoop—they should be taut. Straight-stitch over all heavy design lines except bars, as for the border.

Padstitch with a small zigzag stitch (length 2, width 1) over straight stitching. Cut away the marked open areas of the design and the edges with embroidery or

appliqué scissors, taking care not to cut the stabilizer.

To stitch Richelieu bars (those bars across cut areas), mark their position onto the stabilizer. Padstitch with three rows of short straight stitches (length 1) beside each other over the length of the bar. Satin-stitch the bars, covering the padstitching.

Satin-stitch over remaining design. Be sure to cover all padstitching with satin stitching. Layer the stitching lines—stitch underneath design lines first, then subsequent layers—and stitch over both ends of the Richelieu bars to secure them.

Stitch remaining fine design lines with a short (length 2) triple-straight-stitch. Pull ends of threads through to the back and tie them off.

VARIATIONS

To make napkin ring, reduce motif on a photocopy machine to 60 percent. Mark design onto linen. Fuse 4 layers of stabilizer together and place on wrong side of linen. Place remaining layer on top and place sandwich in hoop. Follow instructions for stitching cutwork motif. Starch well and stitch or glue to purchased napkin ring.

To make bag, lay completed square wrong side up with motif corner at top. Fold side corners to center of square, overlap slightly and hand-sew together. Fold lower corner up and overlap center. Hand-sew in place at center and side edges. Fold motif corner down for top flap.

FINISHING

Gently tear away and remove excess stabilizer. Soak linens in cold water for 5 to 15 minutes. Roll in a towel to absorb excess moisture. Press right side down on a well-padded surface with a pressing cloth while still damp. Starch if desired.

Once Upon a Christening

A variety of heirloom sewing techniques add to the delicate beauty of an enchanting christening gown that is destined to be passed down for generations to come.

SIZE

Baby size 6 months

MATERIALS

Note: All materials are white.

- 2¹/₂ yd. (2.3 m) Swiss batiste
- ¹/₂ yd. (.5 m) Swiss embroidered insertion lace 1" (25 mm) wide
- ¹/₂ yd. (.5 m) Swiss embroidered beading lace ¹/₂" (13 mm) wide
- 2 yd. (1.85 m) edging lace ³/₄" (20 mm) wide
- 5¹/₂ yd. (5 m) edging lace 2³/₄" (70 mm) wide
- 1 yd. (1 m) entredeux ¹/₈" (3 mm) wide
- 3¹/₂ yd. (3.2 m) entredeux ¹/₄" (6 mm) wide
- 1¹/₂ yd. (1.4 m) satin ribbon ¹/₈" (3 mm) wide
- 16 small satin bows with pearl centers
- 3 pearl shank buttons, 7 mm in diameter
- Fine (60 wt.) cotton thread
- Perlé cotton #5

- Water-soluble marking pen
- 2.0/80 double needle
- 7-groove pin tuck foot, embroidery foot, edgestitch foot, buttonhole foot, zipper foot
- Spray starch

CUTTING

Note: Prewash batiste with mild soap flakes and warm water. Press while still slightly damp and lightly starch. Draw a thread across one end of the fabric and straighten the grain. Press and starch all laces.

Pattern pieces on pages 125-126 include ¹/₄" (6 mm) or ¹/₂" (1.3 cm) seam allowances where appropriate.

Batiste

Cut 2 back yokes.
Cut 2 sleeves.
Cut 2 skirts (front and back), each 35" x 41¹/₂" (89 cm x 105 cm).
Cut 2 front yoke center panels, each 3" x 4" (7.5 cm x 10 cm).
Cut 2 front yoke side panels each, 1¹/₂" x 4" (4 cm x 10 cm).

With zipper foot and a narrow zigzag, roll and whip seam edge. Cut entredeux/insertion piece into 3 equal lengths.

Lay yoke pieces on work surface in following order: Place a length of entredeux/insertion in center, scalloped panels on each side with scallop points facing center, entredeux/insertion to both sides, then side panels at each end. Roll and whip all pieces together

Center front yoke pattern over stitched fabric and cut out. Roll and whip ¹/₄" (6 mm) wide entredeux to lower edge of front yoke.

NECK

Roll and whip front yoke and back yoke together at shoulders with ¹/₄" (6 mm) entredeux between. Stitch entredeux to lower edges of back yoke same as for front. Cut a 14" (35.5 cm) piece of ¹/₈" (3 mm) wide entredeux. Trim fabric from one side close to beading. Cut a 29" (73.5 cm) piece of narrow edging lace. Pull a thread in the heading to gather lace to same length as entredeux.

FRONT YOKE

On front yoke center panels, using water-soluble marker, transfer small scalloped pin tuck design (page 126) to vertical center. Mark one row ¹/₂" (1.3 cm) from each side of center row. With double needle, open embroidery foot, and machine set for straight stitch, work pin tucks along marked lines. Trim to 2³/₈" (6 mm) wide, with tucks centered.

Cut 2 pieces of ¹/₄" (6 mm) wide entredeux and 1 piece of Swiss embroidered insertion lace each 12" (30.5 cm) long.

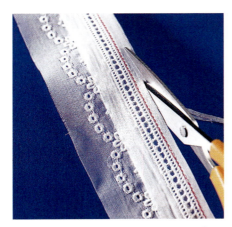

With a short straight stitch, and matching raw edges, stitch entredeux to both sides of insertion lace. Trim close to stitching.

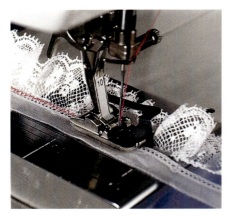

With edgestitch foot and a short zigzag stitch, sew gathered lace to trimmed edge of entredeux. Needle should fall into entredeux beading on one swing and into lace on opposite swing as shown. Adjust lace gathers during stitching. Stitch entredeux and lace to neck edge, beginning and ending 5/8" (1.5 cm) from each end.

SLEEVES

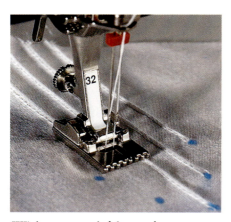

With water-soluble marker, transfer markings for pin tucks to each sleeve. With double needle and pin tuck foot, stitch center pin tuck. Stitch remaining pin tucks to each side between markings, using end groove as a guide. Draw thread ends to wrong side, tie off.

Cut 2 pieces of Swiss embroidered beading lace 6¹/2" (16.3 cm) long, and 2 pieces of narrow edging lace 14" (35.5 cm long). Draw up thread in edging lace and gath-

er to same length as beading. Trim fabric from one edge of beading. With edgestitch foot and narrow zigzag, stitch gathered lace to trimmed edge of beading. Stitch 2 rows of gathering stitches (long straight stitches) close to lower sleeve edges. Gather sleeves to same length as beading. Roll and whip lower edges of sleeves to untrimmed edges of beading.

SKIRT

Mark and cut sleeve openings at side edges of skirt front and back. Stitch one side of skirt back to skirt front with a French seam or overcast edge seam. With disappearing marker, mark one row of large scallops (template, page 126) for center row of curved pin tucks on skirt 6" (15 cm) above lower edge. Mark a vertical line 1" (2.5 cm) above and below the intersection of each scallop for pivot point. Mark hem of skirt with scallops in same manner.

Thread perlé cotton up through needle-plate hole for corded pin tucks. With double needle, pin tuck foot and straight stitch, work pin tucks along marked line. Work 2 more rows of pin tucks on each side of first pin tuck, using outer groove on foot as a guide.

Trim hem edge of skirt along marked scallop line. Roll and whip

1/4" (6 mm) entredeux to hem. Trim remaining edge of entredeux. Gather wide edging lace by pulling a thread in the heading. With edgestitch foot and zigzag stitch, sew lace to trimmed edge of entredeux, adjusting gathers of lace while stitching. Stitch remaining side seam with French seam or overcast edge seam. Mark center of top edge of skirt back. Mark 4" (10 cm) vertical line for back opening. Cut along marked line. Cut a 8" (20 cm) piece of narrow edging lace. With right sides together, stitch lace along both sides of opening. Fold lace to inside on left side to form facing. Stitch diagonally across folded edge of lace.

ASSEMBLY

Press center back yoke edges 3/4" (2 cm) to wrong side twice for facing. Sew 2 rows of gathering stitches (long stitch length) close to upper edges of front and back skirt. Gather along bobbin thread to fit yokes. With zipper foot, roll and whip skirts to beading at front and back yokes. Stitch sleeve underarm seams together. Matching center sleeve pin tucks with center of shoulder, stitch sleeves in place.

FINISHING

Mark and stitch 3 buttonholes 3/8" (1 cm) long on left back yoke, with upper and lower buttonholes 1/4" (6 cm) from upper and lower edges, and remaining buttonhole centered between. Sew buttons on right back yoke, opposite buttonholes.

Beginning at center top of sleeve, thread ribbon through beading on sleeves. Sew a pearled bow to center front of neck and to top of each hem scallop.

Treasured Memories Wall Hanging

Patchwork and quilting form the background canvas of the perfect gift to commemorate that special occasion (ours was made for a wedding). Machine monogramming and decorative collectibles make this a very personal tribute.

SIZE

Wall hanging is 21" x 31" (53.5 cm x 78.5 cm) before framing

MATERIALS

- ■ 1/4 yd. (.25 m) each of ivory damask, ivory moiré taffeta, and white satin
- ■ 1/2 yd. (.50 m) white damask
- ■ 24" x 36" (61 cm x 91.5 cm) piece muslin for backing
- ■ Metallic gold machine embroidery thread
- ■ Matching sewing threads
- ■ Low-loft quilt batting
- ■ Assorted ribbons, braids, beaded lace trims, tassels, buttons, ribbon roses and leaves, dried flowers, and wedding collectibles as desired
- ■ 1 yd. (1 m) ombre wire-edged ribbon 1" (25 mm) wide
- ■ Spray starch
- ■ Patchwork presser foot, walking foot, and embroidery presser foot
- ■ Stabilizer
- ■ Small piece of cardboard
- ■ White craft glue

CUTTING

Note: Patterns on page 127 include 1/4" (6 mm) seam allowance.

White damask

Cut 4 sashing strips each 2½" x 9" (6.5 cm x 23 cm). Cut 3 strips each 2½" x 28½" (6.5 cm x 72 cm) for borders and sashing.

Cut 2 side border strips each 2½" x 22½" (6.5 cm x 57 cm).

Ivory damask

Cut 6 of pattern A square and 12 of pattern B square (page 127).

Ivory moiré taffeta

Cut 50 of pattern C triangle (page 127).

White satin

Cut 50 of pattern C triangle (page 127) and one 6" (15 cm) square.

PIECING

Note: Treat fabric pieces with spray starch before stitching for ease in handling.

With patchwork foot, join taffeta and satin triangles to make squares. Following Wall Hanging Block Diagram, join squares into strips, then join strips to make block. Make 6 blocks.

ASSEMBLY

Join blocks into 2 rows of 3 blocks each with short sashing strips between each block; join rows with a long sashing strip. Stitch remaining long sashing strips to top and bottom of quilt. Stitch a border strip to each side of quilt.

QUILTING

Lay muslin backing on work surface. Center batting on backing, then place quilt top, right side up, on top. Beginning at center, baste layers together. With walking foot, machine-quilt in-the-ditch around A pieces and around each sashing strip.

MACHINE EMBROIDERY

Stabilize satin square following manufacturer's instructions. Attach embroidery foot and set for monogramming. With metallic thread, stitch names and date in center of square.

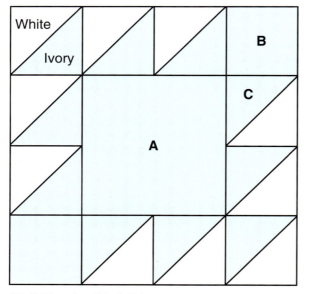

Wall Hanging Block Diagram

Trim cardboard into an oval slightly larger than embroidered area. Trim embroidered piece 1/2" (1.3 cm) larger than cardboard. Run a line of gathering stitches close to edges of fabric. Place fabric over cardboard and gather to fit. Secure threads. Glue lace around the edge, and glue ribbon roses to the front as desired.

Mark position for beads and buttons. By hand, make several backstitches at marked positions and sew beads and buttons in place. Make only as many stitches as needed to secure. Sew-through buttons can be sewn by machine; follow the instructions in your manual.

FINISHING

Trim batting and backing even with quilt top. Plan positions of trims and collectibles on quilt top.

Pin lace appliqués in desired position. With needle and thread, make small running stitches around lace edges, catching base fabric as you sew.

To prepare dried flowers, trim stalks to 6" (15 cm). Hold flowers together and place 1" (2.5 cm) of ribbon beside bottom of stalks. Wind ribbon around bottom of stems, covering raw edge. Continue winding tightly upward to base of flowers. Trim ribbon and glue end in place. Tie remaining ribbon around top of stalk and trim ends diagonally. Sew on wall hanging. Mount and frame wall hanging as desired.

Victorian Bandboxes

With their ribbons and tassels, lush fabrics and embroidery, these lavish cache boxes are opulent enough to hold the crown jewels . . . or a precious lock of hair. Adapt the instructions to fit any bandbox.

SIZE

Blue and green boxes are 6" (15 cm) in diameter, rose box is 8" (20.5 cm) in diameter

MATERIALS

Note: Materials and instructions are for a set of 3 boxes.

All Boxes
- 1½ yds. (1.4 m) cream moiré
- ½ yd. (.5 m) flat gold braid
- Quilt batting
- Tear-away stabilizer
- Fusible web
- Tracing paper
- White craft glue
- Seam sealant
- Pencil and ruler
- Embroidery foot

Green Box
- Cardboard bandbox 6" (15 cm) in diameter x 3¼" (8.2 cm) tall
- ¼ yd. (.25 m) green satin
- 1 yd. (1 m) green decorative rayon cord
- 3½ yds. (3.2 m) woven floral ribbon ⅞" (22 mm) wide
- 1½ yds. (1.4 m) olive satin ribbon ⅝" (15 mm) wide
- 2½ yds. (2.3 m) dark green satin ribbon ¼" (6 mm) wide
- 1 each of olive and dark green rayon tassels 4" (10 cm) long
- Green and purple rayon machine embroidery thread

Blue Box
- Cardboard bandbox 6" (15 cm) in diameter x 3¼" (8.2 cm) tall
- ¼ yd. (.25 m) blue satin
- 1 yd. (1 m) decorative rayon cord
- ¾ yd. (.75 m) woven floral ribbon ¾" (20 mm) wide
- 2 yds. (2 m) light blue satin ribbon ⅜" (10 mm) wide
- 2 yds. (2 m) dark blue satin rib-

bon ⅛" (3 mm) wide
- 1 each of light blue and medium blue rayon tassels 4" (10 cm) long
- Light blue and medium blue rayon machine embroidery thread

Rose Box
- Cardboard bandbox 8" (20.5 cm) in diameter x 4" (10 cm) tall
- ¼ yd. (.25 m) rose satin
- ½ yd. (.5 m) rose decorative rayon cord
- 1½ yds. (1.4 m) woven floral ribbon ¾" (20 mm) wide
- 1½ yds. (1.4 m) pink pom-pom trim
- 2¼ yds. (2.1 m) dark rose satin ribbon ⅝" (15 mm) wide
- 2 rose rayon tassels 4" (10 cm) long
- Pink and dark rose rayon machine embroidery thread
- Fusible tape

CUTTING

Green Box
Cream moiré

Cut a 11" x 20½" (28 cm x 52 cm) topper.

Cut a 5" x 19" (12.5 cm x 48 cm) side cover.

Cut a 3" x 19" (7.5 cm x 48 cm) lining.

Cut 3 circles each 5¾" (14.5 cm) in diameter for base, lid lining, and base lining.

Green satin

Cut a 7½" x 20½" (19 cm x 52 cm) topper lining.

Stabilizer

Cut an 11" x 20½" (28 cm x 52 cm) topper backing.

Batting

Cut a circle 6" (15 cm) in diameter.

Blue Box
Cream moiré

Cut a 9" x 20½" (23 cm x 52 cm) topper.

Cut a 5" x 19" (12.5 cm x 48 cm) side cover.

Cut a 3" x 19" (7.5 cm x 48 cm) lining.

Cut 3 circles each 5¾" (14.5 cm) in diameter for base, lid lining, and base lining.

Blue satin

Cut a 6¼" x 20½" (16 cm x 52 cm) topper lining.

Stabilizer

Cut a 9" x 20½" (23 cm x 52 cm) topper backing.

Batting

Cut a circle 6" (15 cm) in diameter.

Rose Box
Cream moiré

Cut a 10¼" x 26½" (26 cm x 67.5 cm) topper.

Cut a 3½" x 25" (9 cm x 63.5 cm) lining.

Cut 2 circles each 7¾" (19.5 cm) in diameter for lid lining and base lining.

Rose Satin

Cut a 6½" x 26½" (16.5 cm x 67.5 cm) topper lining.

Cut a 5¾" x 25¼" (14.5 cm x 64 cm) side cover.

Cut a circle 7¾" (19.5 cm) in diameter for base.

Stabilizer

Cut a 10¼" x 26½" (26 cm x 67.5 cm) topper backing.

Batting

Cut a circle 8" (20.5 cm) in diameter.

PREPARATION

If box lid is snug fitting, remove enough layers of paper or cardboard from inside rim to accommodate added fabric. Following manufacturer's instructions, apply fusible web to all fabric pieces, except toppers and topper linings. This will prevent edges from fraying. Glue batting to top of lid.

EMBELLISHING BOX BOTTOMS

Lay moiré side cover strip lengthwise on work surface.

Green Box: With pencil and ruler, lightly mark ribbon position from upper to lower edges at 1" (2.5 cm) vertical intervals. Cut olive and dark green ribbons as necessary to 5" (12.5 cm) lengths. Glue ribbons alternately to marked lines, centering the ribbons on the lines.

Blue Box: With pencil and ruler, lightly mark ribbon position from upper to lower edges at 3/4" (2 cm) vertical intervals. Cut light and dark blue ribbons as necessary to 5" (12.5 cm) lengths. Glue ribbons alternately to marked lines, centering the ribbons on the lines.

Rose Box: Cover box with moiré (see Covering Bottoms, right) before applying ribbons. Cut a piece of floral ribbon and 2 pieces of dark rose ribbon each 25 1/4" (64 cm) long. Glue one rose ribbon around lower edge, then glue floral ribbon lapped over it, 1/4" (6 mm) above lower edge. Glue remaining rose ribbon 1 5/8" (4 cm) above lower edge.

COVERING BOTTOMS

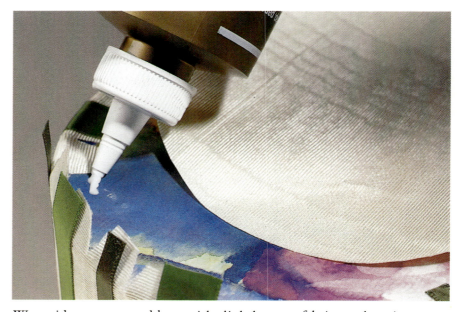

Wrap side cover around box, with slightly more fabric overhanging at top than at base. Glue in place at upper and lower edges of side. Clip base overhang at 1" (2.5 cm) intervals to make tabs. Clip tabs into triangles to eliminate bulk. Do not cut closer than 1/8" (3 mm) from box edge. Turn tabs to base and glue in place. Clip upper overhang at 1" (2.5 cm) intervals. To ease in fullness, first glue one tab on each side of box to inside, stretching slightly, then glue tabs halfway between. Glue remaining tabs in place, easing in fullness. Glue all ribbon ends in place.

Glue linings inside boxes, working from bottom edge up and covering all ribbon and tab ends. Trim one base lining to fit inside box. Glue in place, working 1/4 circle at a time. Glue base in place on box bottom.

MACHINE EMBROIDERY

Lay moiré topper lengthwise on work surface. With pencil and ruler, mark a line 1¹/₂" (3.8 cm) from lower edge of topper. Mark for placement of braid and/or embroidery from top of lower marked line. Lay stabilizer beneath moiré. With embroidery thread and machine embroidery foot, work satin stitch (narrowly spaced zigzag) and/or scallop stitch on marked lines. Test on scrap fabric first. When embroidery is completed, remove excess stabilizer following manufacturer's instructions.

Green Box: Mark vertical lines at 1" (2.5 cm) intervals. With fusible tape, fuse floral ribbon to alternate lines.

With purple thread, work scallops along ribbon edges as shown.

With green thread, satin-stitch remaining lines.

Blue Box: Mark diagonal grid lines 1¹/₈" (2.8 cm) apart. Satin-stitch every other line in each direction with dark blue, then remaining lines with light blue.

Rose Box: Mark vertical lines from top to lower edge at 2" (5 cm) intervals. With pink thread, satin-stitch along marked lines. With dark rose thread, stitch scallops on both sides of satin stitch, with scallop points meeting satin stitch.

TOPPERS

Baste pom-pom trim to one long edge of rose box topper. With right sides together, stitch toppers to topper linings along upper edges. Press seam to inside, then open piece again. Sew moiré and satin side seam. Fold contrast satin to inside and press. Test fit on box lid. Topper should fit snug. Adjust if necessary. Glue topper over lid and to inside of rim. Glue lid lining in place, covering raw edges of topper.

Green Box: Cut a piece of floral ribbon and 2 pieces of dark green ribbon each 20¹/₂" (52 cm) long. Glue or fuse green ribbon to either side of floral ribbon and glue around lid rim.

Blue Box: Cut a 20¹/₂" (52 cm) piece of floral ribbon and glue around lid rim.

Rose Box: Cut a piece of floral and dark rose ribbon each 26¹/₂" (67.5 cm) long. Glue or fuse rose ribbon to one side of floral ribbon and glue in place around lid rim.

FINISHING

Following manufacturer's instructions, apply seam sealant to all raw fabric and ribbon ends.

For green and blue boxes, slip one tassel on each end of cord. Fold cord end up to form a 1" loop and glue in place. Wrap and glue gold braid around cord to secure and cover end. Add extra batting inside green topper for added height. Adjust gathers of top and tie with a length of thread. Tie cords around toppers.

For rose box, slip tassel loop over end of cord and wrap with gold braid. Glue in place.

TIPS

• Before adding tassels to cord, tie them in place to test the length. Trim cord if necessary.

• You can adapt these instructions for any size or shape box. Be sure to measure carefully and add at least ¹/₂" (1.3 cm) overlap at sides, and top and bottom edges.

Keepsake Frame

Whimsical yo-yo puffs, made from gathered circles of fabric, are dressed up in moiré and satin, smothered in pearl buttons, and surrounded with lace to create a frame for a treasured photograph.

SIZE

Frame is 10½" (26.5 cm) tall

MATERIALS

- 8" x 10" (20.5 cm x 25 cm) oval frame covering kit
- ½ yd. (.5 m) cream moiré
- Scraps of cream satin or silk
- 1 yd. (1 m) pregathered cream gauze edging 1" (25 mm) wide
- 1 yd. (1 m) cream pearl-and-lace edging ½" (13 mm) wide
- 1 yd. (1 m) cream rayon cord with header
- Low-loft quilt batting
- A variety of pearl buttons in assorted sizes
- White craft glue or hot glue gun
- Cream sewing thread
- Cream carpet or buttonhole thread

CUTTING

Cream moiré

Frame coverings according to manufacturer's instructions.

3 circles each 4" (10 cm) in diameter.

Cream satin or silk

2 circles each 5½" (14 cm) in diameter.

FRAME

Following manufacturer's instructions, apply batting to frame and cover frame components with moiré. Glue pregathered lace around inner edge of inner opening. Glue cord to outer edge of frame; cover cord edge with pearl-lace trim.

MAKING YO-YOS

Make a gathering stitch (straight stitch with long stitch length) ¼" (6 mm) inside outer edge of each circle.

To gather circles, pull bobbin thread ends and push fabric along thread, adjusting fullness evenly around. Continue to gather until fabric is tight at center. Tie all four thread ends together and trim.

EMBELLISHING FRAME

Position yo-yos on top of frame as desired with gathered sides facing up. Glue in place or stitch with small slipstitches. Glue or stitch large buttons to centers of yo-yos to cover raw edges. Trim some yo-yos with pregathered lace if desired.

To stitch large buttons in place, pass a length of carpet or buttonhole thread through one buttonhole, through the fabric and out through the remaining hole. Tie thread ends with a double knot and trim ends to ¼" (6 mm). Place small buttons below yo-yos and tie in place in same manner.

CHAPTER 3

Dolls That Delight

In every childhood there is a favorite doll or soft toy that is cherished above others. It may be funny, or sweet, or homely—some may think it ugly—but it is loved as the dearest friend. The craft of dollmaking has changed little through the ages. What has changed are the materials available for imparting a doll with a personality of its own or with that of its creator. Purchased or iron-on facial features, synthetic hair, and movable joints offer more options for designing that special friend. With a touch of imagination and some ingenuity, you can make the four charmers in this chapter come alive for the doll lovers in your life.

The Basics

Making dolls and soft toys can be creatively stimulating as well as technically chal lenging. While dollmaking techniques are not difficult, they do require careful atten- tion to details and some special accessories. Read through this section before you begin.

Tools of the Trade

To make cloth dolls or toys, you'll need basic sewing supplies and a few specialized items that will make the crafting easier and the results more polished.

CUTTING

Sharp dressmaking shears. They should be the standard 8" (20.5 cm) length, with good quality blades and comfortable handles.

Embroidery scissors. Choose small scissors with sharp points.

Paper scissors. Use for cutting patterns.

MARKING

No. 2 lead pencils. These work well for marking stitch details,

such as darts, on muslin.

Iron-on transfer marking pen or pencil. Use for transferring facial features onto fabric.

Dressmaker's carbon and trac- ing wheel. This is the traditional method of marking. Follow manu- facturer's instructions for use.

Disappearing markers. Pens or pencils that air-fade or are water- soluble.

NEEDLES AND PINS

Straight pins and safety pins. These are useful for both regular sewing and for holding body pieces in place during stitching.

Needles. Have a variety of sizes on hand, including small darning needles, heavy-duty button and carpet thread needles, and large

stuffed-toy needles for sewing through limbs. Use an embroidery needle if you plan to hand-embroi- der faces.

THREADS

All-purpose sewing thread. Use good quality thread for all hand and machine sewing.

Decorative threads. Choose rayons, silks, and metallics, for example, to machine-embroider faces or embellish clothes.

Embroidery floss or perlé cot- ton. Use for hand embroidery on faces and clothing.

Buttonhole twist or carpet thread. This is heavier and stronger than regular thread and is best for sewing limbs and sculpting faces.

STABILIZERS

When working with fine fabrics, add a backing so that the fabric will feed evenly and not bunch during decorative-stitching or embroidering. Use also to provide a sturdy backing when machine-embroidering faces or decorative edgings and motifs onto fabric. Use tissue paper, freezer paper, or purchased wash-away, tear-away, iron-away, or liquid stabilizers. Follow manufacturer's instructions for the best results.

GLUES AND FUSIBLES

Fusible web. Use paper-backed fusibles to join two layers of fabric together. This will help stop raw, cut edges from fraying, and hold appliqués in place for stitching.
Fusible tape. Use for fusing ribbons and trims in place or for holding them securely for sewing.
Craft glue. Use a tacky white craft glue that dries clear for gluing hair and embellishments in place. A glue gun may also be useful.

MACHINE SEWING

Be sure your machine is in top working order and a new needle is inserted before beginning a new project. Make full use of the decorative stitch capabilities of your machine and incorporate techniques you have learned in other areas, such as quilting, appliqué, machine embroidery, and pin tucks. A patchwork presser foot will help for sewing uniform seams with $1/4"$ (6 mm) seam allowances.

STUFFING

Turning tool. Use a turning tool, such as Fasturn®, to turn small pieces of sewn-together fabric, such as arms or legs, to the right side.
Pointed tool. Necessary to push out corners or small sculptural areas, such as fingers. A knitting needle works well.
Stuffing tool. A purchased stuffing tool, such as Stuff-It, or a narrow dowel, knitting needle, chopstick, or skewer is useful for pushing stuffing firmly into body parts. Stuffing tweezers are also helpful for filling out tight areas.

MAKING FACES

Note: If the doll or toy is for a young child, do not use items that can be pulled off and swallowed. In such cases it is best to embroider or paint facial features.

Embroidered faces. If worked by machine, use cotton, rayon, or decorative threads. Use embroidery floss or perlé cotton for hand-embroidering.

Painted faces. Fabric paints adhere well, are easy to use, and come in a variety of colors and finishes, including matte, shiny, metallic, iridescent, and glitter. Acrylic paints will also work on fabric. Have a variety of brushes on hand.

Drawn faces. Use permanent fabric markers for strong features or outlines. For a softer, more muted look use colored pencils or crayons.

Iron-on faces. These are either included with a doll pattern or purchased separately. They are either transfers or fusible embroidered face parts. Iron-on transferable faces can be highlighted with pencils, paints, or blush after they have been applied. Follow manufacturer's instructions carefully for best results.

Purchased face parts. Doll and animal eyes are available in a variety of styles, colors, and sizes. Buttons can also be used for eyes. Bear muzzles, noses, mouths, and whiskers are available from doll specialists. Facial features can also be cut from fabric or felt and glued or fused in place.

Cosmetics. Powdered blush adds color to cheeks.

Materials

Let the pattern and your imagination help with the selection of materials. There are no hard-and-fast rules, but you may want to follow these suggestions until you gain more confidence.

DOLL BODIES

Unbleached muslin is an excellent choice for body fabric. It is 100 percent cotton, making it easy to sew and press, and it can be dyed to any skin shade. Use fabric dyes—water them down or mix them for interesting tint variations—or use tea for a traditional or antiqued look (see Preparing the Fabric, this page). Flesh-colored cotton fabric is another good choice, or use an unusual color to create an interesting effect. Flesh-colored stretch fabrics specifically for dollmaking are also available.

DOLL CLOTHES

There is no limit to the fabrics you can use to make clothes for dolls. Cotton print fabrics, like those used by quilters, provide you with a wide variety of prints and colors, including reproduction prints. Solids and small-scale prints work well for most doll clothes. For more elaborate costumes, experiment with remnants of decorative fabrics, such as velvets, linens, taffetas, satins, and laces.

STUFFED TOYS

If the toy will be handled by a child, choose medium-weight washable fabrics or fake furs. For decorative toys, choose any light-to medium-weight fabric. Just be sure it is opaque and has a stable weave.

HAIR

All sorts of materials can be used to create hair that either looks realistic or has a whimsical quality. For a more natural-looking coif, choose wool roving, worsted-weight wool yarn, flax, and unraveled rope. Packaged hair is available in many styles and in an array of colors. If your doll is more for fun than realism, try nontraditional colors or a combination of colors to create a distinctive personality. Colorful novelty yarns, metallics, mohairs, and bouclés have textural appeal. Mix strands of embroidery floss or interesting threads, or use raffia or torn strips of fabric for a rustic look.

EMBELLISHMENTS

Use whatever you can find or have in your collection—buttons and ribbons, charms and laces, ribbon roses, embroidered appliqués, bows and beads, braids and baubles. Let your imagination soar!

STUFFING

The choice of stuffing plays a major role in the finished look of your doll. Experiment with different varieties to find the one you prefer to work with. Polyester fiberfill and uncarded wool are the most frequently used. You may also recycle old pantyhose or fabric scraps. Dolls and toys that are to be loosely stuffed can be filled with stuffing pellets.

Making the Doll or Toy

PREPARING FABRIC

To begin, choose the fabric you want to use for your doll's body. Prewash and press all fabrics before cutting to shrink and remove sizing, especially if the doll, toy, or clothes will be washed. If the fabric skin shade you desire is not available, dye muslin or another light-colored fabric with fabric dyes or with tea for an aged look. Follow package directions for using fabric dye.

If using tea, simply brew a quart (1 liter) of very strong tea with 8 or 9 tea bags. Stir the mixture occasionally while it brews so that the color will be even. Remove bags and soak fabric in the tea until it is slightly darker than the desired shade (fabric will lighten as it dries). Dry fabric in a dryer or press while damp to set the color.

Before cutting out pattern pieces, plan how you want to make the face. Transfer the face pattern piece onto the fabric and either paint or embroider it. The extra fabric will allow you to tape the face in place while you are working. Wait until the head is stuffed to add highlights with powdered blush. If embroidering, you may wish to place the piece in an embroidery hoop.

If you're embroidering on a light-colored fabric, an easy way to conceal thread ends is to work through two layers of fabric. When the stitching is complete, cut out the head along marked lines, through both layers, adding any pattern markings.

TRANSFERRING PATTERNS

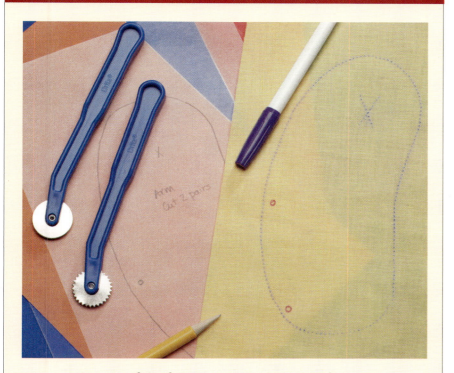

Use one of the following methods to transfer pattern outlines to fabric. Patterns in this book are full size and include 1/4" (6 mm) seam allowances.

- Photocopy patterns directly from the source and cut them out. This is particularly useful when patterns need to be enlarged.

- Place dressmaker's carbon paper under the pattern pieces on the wrong side of the fabric. Use a tracing wheel to transfer the outline. This method is more successful for large, less detailed shapes.

- Tracing can be done over a light box or a sunny window. Tape the pattern to the light source, then tape the fabric, wrong side facing up, over the pattern. Use a No. 2 lead mechanical pencil or dressmaker's marker to trace the pattern lines. Don't use an

air-fading disappearing marker unless you plan to cut out and assemble your doll within 24 hours. Follow manufacturer's directions when using markers. Always test first.

- Trace pattern pieces onto tracing paper, cut them out, then pin them to fabric and cut out.

- Use chalk or a marker to add any pattern markings after cutting out pieces from fabric.

- To mark face details, trace the features onto tracing paper with an iron-on transfer marking pen or pencil. Place the tracing face down on the fabric and press with an iron. To avoid smudges, do not move the iron around. Test on scrap fabric first to ensure markings will remove easily.

ASSEMBLY

Stitch body pieces in the order specified in your pattern or project instructions. Dolls are usually made with a 1/4" (6 mm) seam allowance. Check individual instructions before sewing. When sewing, use a small stitch with a short length to increase the strength of the seams, and remember to leave openings for turning. Trim seams to about 1/8" (3 mm) along curved edges. At angled sections, such as the junction of the neck and shoulders, clip seams close to the stitching line. Turn right side out through openings.

STUFFING

One of the most crucial steps in the creation of your doll or toy is the stuffing process. Use a stuffing tool or substitute a chopstick, dowel, or wooden skewer to push stuffing into the doll. Work with very small amounts of stuffing at a time, beginning at the outside edges of each piece and working toward the center. When a piece is stuffed, whipstitch the opening closed before proceeding to the next piece, unless the pattern directions indicate otherwise.

Join the limbs to the body as indicated in your pattern directions; this can be done by sewing with a large stuffed-toy needle through the body, with purchased doll joints, or with buttons. Don't use buttons for joining limbs if the doll or toy is for a small child.

If required, hand- or machine-stitch through joints, such as at elbows or knees, after stuffing. Sculpt the face with a large needle and buttonhole thread following pattern instructions.

STITCHING SMALL SECTIONS

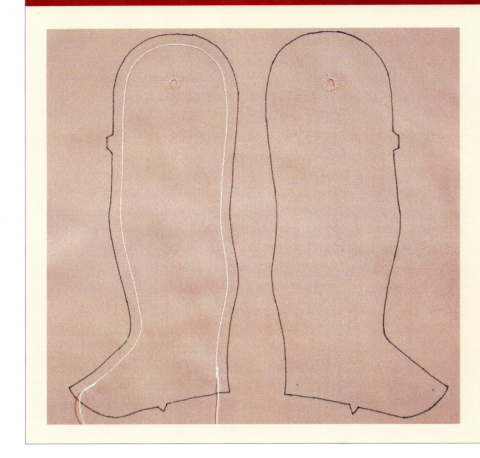

When stitching small pieces together, such as arms and legs, it is frequently easier to stitch them before you cut them out. Simply trace the relevant pattern pieces and any pattern markings onto the wrong side of the fabric, leaving at least 1/2" (1.3 cm) between them.

Place another piece of fabric behind this one, with right sides together. Stitch 1/4" (6 mm) inside the marked lines, leaving openings for turning where instructed. Use a patchwork foot for an accurate 1/4" (6 mm) seam allowance. Cut out pieces along marked lines and turn right side out.

This method is also helpful when making several toys at one time.

HAIR

Working with the fiber you've chosen for the doll's hair, decide on the hairstyle you'd like for your doll. The fastest and easiest way to secure hair in place is with craft glue. This works particularly well with curly hair or with styles requiring minimum styling. Work over small sections of the head at one time, and wait until one area is dry before proceeding to another. Use only enough glue to secure the bottom layers of the hair in place, otherwise it will become stiff and hard to style.

If you'd like your doll to have a part in his or her hair, lay out strands of the hair fiber or yarn side by side along a narrow strip of muslin or a piece of twill tape. By machine, with matching thread,

work a straight-stitch part across the center of the strands. Trim the fabric to about 1/4" (6 mm) on each side of the part, then fold half of the hair piece back over the stitched part to expose the muslin base. Stitch through the layers of hair and the muslin base with a 1/8" (3 mm) seam. When you fold back the hair, the part will look quite natural and the original seam will be concealed. Glue the finished hair to the doll's head along the muslin base, and glue or hand-sew in place along the sides and down the back of the head.

An easier method is to lay out the hair on tear-away stabilizer or on transparent tape. Stitch along the part with matching thread and a short stitch length. Place the

tape on one or both sides of the part; don't stitch through it. Remove the stabilizer or the tape. With this method, you will have a visible stitched part in the hair. Glue hair in place.

For a more raggedy homespun look, try making hair from fabric strips. Either knits or woven fabrics work well. Tear the fabric into strips 1/2" (1.3 cm) wide and stitch or glue them in place. You can also cut strips with pinking shears or use a rotary cutter with a pinking blade. Strips can be left long or gathered into ponytails at the side of the head.

Style hair, adding bows, ribbons, or a hat, if desired. You can use hair spray to hold hair in place. Test on scraps of the hair fiber first.

NEW WAVE

Recycle wool from old sweaters or unused skeins into wavy hair for your doll. Simply unravel the yarn from the sweater, cut it to the desired length, and stitch or glue it in place. To use skeins of yarn, knit a swatch, dampen it, and allow it to dry. When the swatch has dried, unravel the yarn, cut it to the desired length, and stitch or glue it in place.

DRESSING UP

Begin with the basic pattern pieces and instructions for your chosen doll, then embellish to your heart's content. Since a doll's clothing is designed for fun or fantasy, almost anything goes when it comes to dressing up the outfit you choose.

Add lots of trims for a fun look. Many ribbons and laces can be glued on for fast application. Check craft stores for miniature accessories such as hats, flowers, bows, baskets, eyeglasses, jewelry and other tiny embellishments.

Look through your work basket for items that can be added to your dolls. Buttons can be used for faces or stitched all over a head as an alternative to hair. Rows of buttons stitched to clothing are also fun. Turn small pieces of fabric or ribbon into yo-yos (see page 57). Make ribbon roses from tiny ribbon scraps.

If your doll or toy is for a small child, don't use buttons for closures, facial features, or as a trim. VELCRO® is a good substitute and is easy for tiny fingers to manipulate. Paint or embroider faces or sew on facial features made from felt or fabric scraps—and be careful with trims, such as pom-poms, that are glued and could be removed easily by a child.

Sweet Sarah

One of our most popular doll designers is Linda Carr, whose beguiling characters have delighted thousands of home sewers. You'll find the following dollmaking tips helpful when you purchase the pattern for Sarah (see page 143).

MATERIALS

- Vogue pattern 8336
- Materials and notions as per pattern envelope
- Paper and protective cloth for ironing board
- Patchwork presser foot

CUTTING

Follow the layout and cutting directions on the pattern instruction sheet.

NOTE

Turn to page 143 for information on ordering your Linda Carr doll pattern. Instructions and an iron-on face are included in the pattern envelope. The following pages include additional tips and techniques to assist you in the construction of the doll.

FACE

Use only 100 percent white polyester fabric for the face. Transfer colors will not show as well on colored fabric. If using knits, use only stable knits, or interface first. Test on a fabric scrap before beginning. Set a dry iron to 350 degrees Fahrenheit (160 degrees Celsius) or to the linen setting. Allow iron to heat fully—if it is not hot enough, the transfer will not take. Do not use steam, the steam jets will leave marks on the face.

Place a protective cover on the ironing board to prevent excess inks from staining. Cut out the transfer and center it face down on the white fabric. Place a clean sheet of paper over the transfer so that the entire ink surface is covered. Press the iron evenly and firmly on the transfer for 30 seconds. Do not move the iron around while it is on the transfer, it will cause the transfer to smudge. Lift the iron and continue to place it around the transfer in a circle. Apply direct, constant heat without scorching the fabric. Allow the transfer to cool for 1 minute before gently removing it from the fabric. Cut out the face.

The transfer can be used 2 or 3 times, but the strength of the color will diminish considerably with each use. Use a permanent marker to outline eyelashes and apply blusher to cheeks to strengthen color. Set with hair spray. You may also use permanent fabric paints to add more color.

To give some dimension to the cheeks of the doll, after the head is stuffed, make a small stitch at the inside corner of one eye. Bring the needle to the outside of the mouth and make another small stitch, pulling the thread slightly. Bring the thread up to the outside corner of the eye, stitch again, pulling thread slightly. Secure thread and repeat for other side of face.

HAIR

Choose worsted-weight wool yarn for the best results. Follow pattern instruction sheet to stitch yarn in place for hair front and bangs.

When winding yarn around cardboard, take care not to pull it taut, so it will not lose its elasticity and shorten when cut.

To stitch hair to the back of the head more easily, press the center back head piece in half lengthwise. Open flat. Working from markings on pattern, lay strands of yarn centered along the foldline in small bunches, about 1" (2.5 cm) at a time. Machine-stitch the hair to the head. Take care not to catch the yarn in the seams when stitching the head pieces together. After head is stuffed, style and braid hair. Trim bangs and ends of braids. Use fabric glue to hold hair in place. Tack braids to side of head if desired.

FEET

When stitching the feet in place, snip the fabric 1/8" (3 mm) into the seam allowance at either side of the center back leg seam. Use a patchwork presser foot to ensure accurate seams.

JOINTS

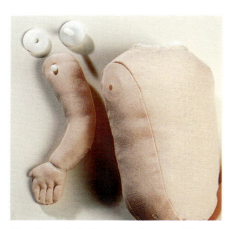

Purchased doll joints inserted into the arms and legs will allow ease of movement. Use the same joints that are commercially available for movable teddy bear limbs. Follow package directions. Once joints are inserted into each other, they cannot be removed. Before stitching arm and leg seams, snip holes in the fabric at the markings on the pattern. It is not necessary to reinforce the openings, but if you prefer to, use a basting or blanket stitch. If your machine has a preset eyelet stitch, this will also work well. If you are using knit fabric for the doll body, you will need to interface the fabric around the holes. Place the shanks in the arms and legs, and the flat disk in the body to prevent limbs from separating with frequent use.

STUFFING

Proper stuffing is essential to create a smooth, firm head and body. Begin by teasing out small amounts of stuffing at a time. Pull in several different directions to make long, loose, flat fibers. Never stuff with balls of fiberfill—these make lumps; and only stuff with small amounts so that beginnings and endings won't be seen.

To stuff the face, lay long, flat patches of stuffing at the base of the chin to fill out and round the face, smoothing in the process to avoid lumps. Add smaller pieces, pushing forward toward the chin to ensure a distinctive chin line and push the gathered section underneath. Push small amounts of stuffing into the chin with a stuffing tool if there are any wrinkles. Continue stuffing until the head is full. Stuff the neck until it is rigid to make sure the head will stay up.

HANDS

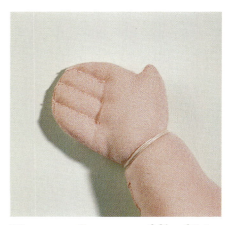

Place a small amount of fiberfill in the hands. Stitch along marked stitching lines. Pull threads to one side and tie off securely. With a pointed stuffing tool or tweezers, stuff small pieces of fiberfill into fingers to fill them out. Continue to stuff the arms until the seams are expanded. To finish hand, wrap wrist several times with thread and secure.

Topsy-Turvy Doll

Topsy-turvy dolls have been teaching children the concept of opposites for generations. Our little lady, with her two outfits and two different expressions, is dressed up and ready both for a day out and to snuggle in for the night.

SIZE

Doll is 15" (38 cm) long

MATERIALS

- ¼ yd. (.25 m) unbleached muslin
- ½ yd. (.5 m) blue cotton print fabric for dress
- ½ yd. (.5 m) white cotton print fabric for nightgown
- 6" x 12" (15 cm x 30.5 cm) piece blue stripe fabric for dress bodice
- ¾ yd. (.75 m) blue satin cording with header
- ¾ yd. (.75 m) blue satin ribbon ¼" (6 mm) wide
- ¾ yd. (.75 m) red picot-edged satin ribbon ⅞" (22 mm) wide
- ½ yd. (.5 m) pregathered white lace ½" (13 mm) wide
- ¾ yd. (.75 m) elastic ¼" (6 mm) wide
- Acrylic paints: light blue, dark blue, brown, pink, red, black, and white
- Fine paintbrush
- No. 2 lead pencil
- Pink coloring pencil
- Polyester fiberfill
- 3 small red heart buttons
- Brown roving
- Sewing threads
- Rayon machine-embroidery threads in red, dark yellow, green, medium blue, dark blue, and silver
- 2 snaps
- Tear-away stabilizer
- Stuffing tool
- Disappearing marker
- Embroidery foot

CUTTING

Note: Prewash and press all fabrics. Patterns on pages 127-128 include ¼" (6 mm) seam allowance. Join pattern pieces as marked.

Muslin
Cut 2 body pieces.
Cut 8 arm pieces.

Blue cotton print
Cut 2 pieces each 4½" x 5" (11.5 cm x 12.5 cm) for sleeves.
Cut 1 piece 10½" x 20" (27 cm x 51 cm) for dress skirt.

Blue stripe
Cut 1 dress bodice front and 2 bodice backs.

White cotton print
Cut 1 nightgown bodice front and 2 bodice backs.
Cut 2 pieces 4½" x 5" (11.5 cm x 12.5 cm) for nightgown sleeves.
Cut 1 piece 10½" x 20" (27 cm x 51 cm) for nightgown skirt.

BODY AND FACE

With pencil, transfer face and arm markings to one body piece. Paint faces as shown, watering down paints and blotting brush, as necessary before applying, for a soft look. Shade eyelids and add blush to cheeks with pink pencil.

With a short stitch length, sew body front to back, right sides together, leaving armhole area open as indicated on pattern. Clip neck curves and trim seams close to stitching. Turn right side out.

With stuffing tool, stuff small amounts of fiberfill into one doll head and neck, packing it firmly. Take extra care to make neck very strong. Repeat for second head; set aside.

ARMS

Sew arms, right sides together, using a short stitch length. Leave shoulder end open. Clip curves and corners and trim seams to ⅛" (3 mm). Turn right side out.

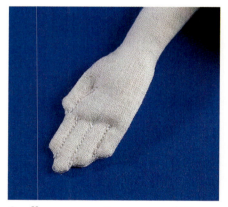

Stuff a very small amount of fiberfill into hand area, flatten, then machine-stitch along finger lines. Lightly stuff arm to elbow; machine-stitch along marked fold-line. Stuff halfway up remaining portion of arm.

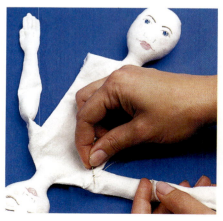

On body, turn arm opening seam allowance to wrong side. Slip arm inside, checking that hand is positioned with thumb up. Slipstitch arm to shoulder area. Flatten upper arm $1/2"$ (1.3 cm) from shoulder, matching seams; hand-sew a shoulder foldline at right angles to elbow seam as shown. Firmly stuff this arm's remaining shoulder area. Attach opposite arm in same manner.

Continue to stuff body, working toward second head. When body is almost completely stuffed, attach third arm as before. Before attaching fourth arm, make sure entire body is firm. Hand-sew last shoulder fold before filling out last shoulder area; close final shoulder seam.

MACHINE EMBROIDERY

Transfer sleeve placement markings and mark center front on all bodices and skirts. Place stabilizer behind pieces. With embroidery thread and embroidery foot, machine-embroider details as follows:

Dress: Turn under narrow hem on sleeve edges. With red thread, embroider scallops along sleeve hems. With yellow thread, stitch 2 vertical rows of scallops $1/2"$ (1.3 cm) from center front. On skirt, with yellow thread, work a row of satin stitches $1 1/2"$ (4 cm)

from lower edge. Work 2 more rows of satin stitching with red and green thread 1" (2.5 cm) above first row. With colors as desired, stitch a row of scallops on either side of satin stitching.

Nightgown: Stitch medium blue scallops on sleeve hems as for dress. On bodice, work a narrow row of silver satin stitches $3/4"$ (2 cm) above lower edge. Stitch medium blue scallops on either side of silver thread. On skirt, work rows of decorative stitching as shown or as desired.

CLOTHING

Sew dress bodice front and back together at shoulders. With matching thread, machine-stitch a narrow hem around neck. Press $1/4"$ (6 mm) under at back openings and topstitch. Lap one edge over the other and baste together along bottom edge.

On wrong side of dress sleeves, with fabric marker, mark a line $3/4"$ (2 cm) from sleeve hem. Place elastic cord on line, tack at one end; zigzag over cord. Draw up elastic until "wrist" measures 2" (5 cm) wide; tack end in place. Cut away remaining elastic. Stitch 2 lines of gathering stitches close to top of sleeve. Draw up gathers. Pin sleeve to bodice between marks, stitch in place. Repeat for opposite sleeve. Fold sleeves and bodices across shoulder line, right sides together and matching bottom raw edges. Stitch side and underarm seams.

With right sides together, stitch short ends of dress skirt together for center back. Stitch 2 lines of

gathering stitches close to top edge. Draw up gathers to fit bodice. Pin skirt to bodice with right sides together and hand-sew in place. Repeat for nightgown. Stitch one long edge of blue cording along hem of dress skirt with edges even. Put one dress inside the other, right sides together, matching center fronts, center

backs, and raw edges. Sew dress and nightgown together at hem, using cord basting as a guide. Turn right side out. Line up waists of the two dresses and hand-sew them together with a short running stitch. Place dress/nightgown on doll. Hand-sew snaps to the back openings of both dress and nightgown.

HAIR

Cut several pieces of roving 12" (30.5 cm) long for upper head hair and back hair. Cut a piece of stabilizer 1" (2.5 cm) wide and 4" (10 cm) long. Center strips of roving on stabilizer and machine-stitch in place down the center, using thread lighter than hair color. Stitch along same line several times. Tear stabilizer away.

With pencil, mark vertical center of top and back of head. Pin hair to head, centering stitching on marked line. For back hair, stitch one piece of roving, folded in half, to a small piece of stabilizer. Remove excess stabilizer as before; glue in place under back of top hair. Glue top hair in place. Style hair and trim ends.

FINISHING

For daytime doll, hand-sew heart buttons to center front of dress bodice. Cut 16" (40.5 cm) length of picot ribbon. Tie into a bow and glue to back of doll's hair. Pull picot thread along one edge of remaining ribbon to gather. Tie around doll's neck.

For nighttime doll, cut pregathered lace into 2 lengths each 3 1/2"

(9 cm). Stitch together along straight edges. Place around doll's neck and whipstitch ends together at back of neck. Cut 14" (35.5 cm) length of 1/4" (6 mm) wide blue

ribbon. Tie around center of lace, making a bow at center front. Stitch remaining lace around gathered portion of each sleeve. Braid hair and tie with remaining blue ribbon.

Raffie, the Scarecrow

This fellow is not likely to scare away any crows, but he is likely to win the hearts of children of all ages. The realistic-looking strawlike effect is achieved by attaching synthetic raffia to twill tape and gluing it in place.

SIZE

Scarecrow is 19" (48.5 cm) tall

MATERIALS

- 1/2 yd. (.5 m) cream cotton fabric
- 1/4 yd. (.25 m) blue and white gingham fabric
- 1/4 yd. (.25 m) blue cotton fabric
- 1/4 yd. (.25 m) sunflower print fabric
- Polyester fiberfill
- Twill tape
- 3 assorted buttons each 1/2" (13 mm) wide
- Synthetic raffia
- Paper-backed fusible web
- White craft glue
- Tear-away stabilizer
- Machine embroidery threads in black, red, gold, and orange
- 1 yd. (1 m) string
- Disappearing fabric marker
- Stuffing tool
- Embroidery foot

CUTTING

Note: Prewash and press all fabrics. Patterns on pages 130-131 include 1/4" (6 mm) seam allowance. Join pattern pieces as marked.

Cream cotton

Cut 2 bodies.

Gingham

Fold fabric in quarters, align jacket pattern on folds as indicated. Cut 1.

Blue cotton

Cut 2 pieces 7" x 10" (8 cm x 25.5 cm) for pants.

Cut 4 1/2" x 8 1/2" (11.5 cm x 21.5 cm) piece for hat lining.

Sunflower print

Cut 4 1/2" x 8 1/2" (11.5 cm x 21.5 cm) piece for hat.

Cut 1 jacket lapel.

Twill tape

Cut 2 lengths each 5 1/2" (14 cm) for arms.

Cut 2 lengths each 6" (15 cm) for legs.

Cut 8" (20.5 cm) length for neck.

Cut 10 1/2" (27 cm) length for head.

FACE AND BODY

Transfer markings for body folds and face to body front. Place stabilizer behind face. With machine embroidery thread and embroidery foot, machine-embroider face with satin stitches. Graduate stitch width from top to bottom of eyes to fill triangle. Tear away stabilizer.

Pin body front to body back with right sides together. Stitch along seamlines, leaving an opening for turning. Clip curves and trim seam close to stitching line at crotch. Turn right side out.

Stuff head, then arms and legs to marked stitching lines. Machine-stitch along marked lines. Stuff to next marked lines, stitch, and complete stuffing. Slipstitch opening closed.

Wrap and tie string around neck, wrists, and ankles for added definition.

TIP

For a more floppy scarecrow, stuff the body with weighted polypropylene stuffing pellets. This will make the doll more flexible and allow it to assume different positions. Fill the head and neck with fiberfill to keep them erect.

JACKET

Trace jacket facing onto paper backing of fusible web and cut out. Following manufacturer's instructions, apply fusible web to back of facing. Transfer center front and neckline markings to facing. Apply facing to wrong side of jacket as shown, lining up center front and neckline. Slit jacket front and cut along neckline to make lapels.

Cut random patch shapes from fusible web; apply to wrong side of various fabric scraps. Cut out and apply to jacket as desired. Machine-embroider around patches with contrasting thread and a triple-zigzag stitch. Satin-stitch contrasting straight lines.

With right sides together, sew side and underarm seams of jacket. Clip underarm curve, turn right side out. Clip $1/2$" (1.3 cm) into sleeve and jacket hems every $1/4$" (6 mm). Tear about 1" (2.5 cm) into jacket and sleeves for fringe. Trim excess threads.

PANTS

Apply and stitch patches same as for jacket. With right sides together, fold each leg in half lengthwise and stitch 5" (12.5 cm) up from hem. With right sides together, place one leg inside the other and stitch crotch seam. Turn right side out. Press $1/2$" (1.3 cm) to wrong side at waistband; clip every $1/4$" (6 mm) along fold. Open out and thread string through slits for drawstring waist. Clip pant hems as for jacket and tear fringe.

TIPS

- After fusing patches, apply zigzags and "stitches" with fabric paint to save sewing time. You can also use fabric paint to outline the print on the fabric and to paint in the facial features.
- For a more rustic scarecrow, use tea-dyed muslin for the body and make the clothing from burlap. Unravel the threads at the hems to make a fringe instead of snipping and tearing the fabric.

RAFFIA TRIM

For arm and leg raffia trim, cut synthetic raffia into 3½" (9 cm) lengths. Lay raffia on twill tape so that edges are slightly uneven. Stitch raffia to twill tape. For the neck, stitch 4" (10 cm) lengths of raffia to 8" (20.5 cm) length of twill tape. For the head, fold raffia pieces in half before stitching onto 10½" (27 cm) length of twill tape.

Pin ½" (1.3 cm) to ¾" (2 cm) of each end of neck strip over shoulders and arrange the rest in a deep, wide U shape across chest. Glue in place. Put head piece aside until hat is completed.

HAT

Right sides together, sew narrow seams in both short ends of fabric rectangles. Turn right side out. Fold hat piece in half, lining facing out and hemmed edges together. Stitch along one edge from fold to seamed edge. Turn seam to inside, creating a triangular cap with one long raw edge. Clip and tear fringe along raw edge same as before. Fold up left edge for brim and position on head for raffia placement. Remove hat and glue head raffia strip in place. Glue hat over raffia. Trim raffia if desired.

FINISHING

Place pants on doll and tie waist. Place jacket on doll, fold lapels back and crease. Overlap front edges about ½" (1.3 cm); pin. Arrange buttons; sew in place on jacket front, catching both layers and sewing jacket closed. Tie a length of raffia around waist and at wrists and ankles, if desired. For a more rustic appearance, use wooden buttons.

Pin arm and leg twill tape strips on doll, adjusting placement so that raffia covers all but last ½" (1.3 cm) of arm and leg; glue in place.

Patches, the Teddy

Our bright and colorful teddy bear pieced from scraps has movable arms and legs, yet is soft and cuddly as a stuffed bear should be. Easy piecing combines fusible techniques with rickrack and machine embellishments.

SIZE

Bear is 18" (46 cm) tall

MATERIALS

- ◾ 5/8 yd. (.6 m) remnants of assorted plaid, gingham, and polka-dot cotton blends
- ◾ 1/4 yd. (.25 m) square muslin
- ◾ 2" (5 cm) square of black felt
- ◾ 1/4 yd. (.25 m) paper-backed fusible web
- ◾ 3" x 6" (7.5 cm x 15 cm) piece batting
- ◾ Red baby rickrack
- ◾ 5/8 yd. (.6 m) blue velvet ribbon 7/8" (22 mm) wide
- ◾ Polyester fiberfill
- ◾ 2 black buttons for eyes, 5/8" (15 mm) in diameter
- ◾ 3 buttons for body, 1/2" (13 mm) in diameter
- ◾ 4 buttons for joints, 5/8" (15 mm) in diameter
- ◾ Red rayon machine embroidery thread
- ◾ Red upholstery thread
- ◾ Embroidery needle
- ◾ Soft-sculpture or upholstery needles
- ◾ Stuffing tool
- ◾ White craft glue
- ◾ Embroidery foot

CUTTING

Note: Prewash and press all fabrics. Patterns on pages 128-129 include 1/4" (6 mm) seam allowance. Join pattern pieces as marked.

Remnants

Back fabrics with fusible web following manufacturer's instructions and cut into straight-sided patches.

Bear

Cut 2 each of body back and front.
Cut 4 each of arms and legs.
Cut 2 soles.
Cut 4 ears.

Muslin

Cut muslin pieces about 1 1/2" (3.8 cm) larger than each pattern piece.

Felt

Cut 1 nose/mouth piece.

Batting

Cut 2 ears.

pieces. Fuse 2 different remnants in place for each arm and use a single piece of fused fabric for backs, soles, and ears.

When pattern outline is completely covered, with rayon machine embroidery thread and embroidery foot, work assorted decorative stitches over raw edges. Cover some edges with rickrack and sew in place with a straight stitch.

Lay pattern pieces onto patchwork fabric and pin in place. Cut out pattern pieces, adding pattern markings where necessary.

BODY

Stitch darts in body fronts. Press to one side. Stitch body front sections together at center front with a 1/4" (6 mm) seam. Baste batting to wrong side of two ear sections. Trim batting close to basting. Stitch remaining ear sections with

PIECING

Trace a rough outline of each body pattern piece to muslin. Fuse first patch to center of muslin.

Continue to fuse remnants to muslin square, each piece slightly overlapping previously fused

right sides together, leaving lower edges open. Turn right side out and press. Baste raw edges together. Baste ears to body front. Stitch darts in body backs. Press open. Stitch body back sections together, leaving an opening in center of seam for turning. With right sides together, pin body front to body back. Adjust ease and stitch. Clip seams at curves. Turn right side out through opening in back.

ARMS AND LEGS

Stitch two arm sections together, leaving an opening between small dots. Turn right side out and press. Stuff arm firmly below button marking and loosely above button marking. Slipstitch opening closed.

Stitch two leg sections together, leaving an opening between small dots and at lower edge. With right sides together, pin a sole to each lower leg and stitch in place, clipping seam allowance where necessary for fit. Turn right side out and press. Stuff leg firmly below button marking and loosely above button marking. Slipstitch opening closed.

TIPS

- If you are making this bear for a small child, do not use buttons. Make the eyes from felt, and to sew the arms and legs in place with embroidery floss, make a neat cross-stitch X on the outside.
- Vary the theme of the bear by using different fabrics. Mix denim with bandana prints, use patches of Ultrasuede® scraps, calicoes, velvets, flannels, taffetas, and Christmas prints. Recycle fabrics from men's ties.

ASSEMBLY

Pin arms to body, matching symbols. Center large button over arm at marking. With upholstery thread, stitch button into place through all thicknesses, leaving some thread ease between arm and body. After several stitches, finish by wrapping thread around thread shank between arm and body. Secure thread on inside of body section. Attach legs to body in same manner.

FINISHING

With stuffing tool, stuff body with fiberfill, using large, flat sections under face to avoid lumps. Pack fiberfill tightly. Slipstitch opening closed.

For eyes, sew buttons to face at markings with soft sculpture needle and upholstery thread. Connect them through head with a single thread. Pull thread tightly to indent face slightly, creating a muzzle. Glue felt nose and mouth to front of face. Sew buttons on front body. Tie ribbon into a bow around neck.

CHAPTER 4

The Urge to Serge

The surge of interest in serging has prompted many home sewers to include the serger as an integral part of their sewing equipment. Sergers allow us to duplicate commercial finishes at home, as well as to speed up the sewing process by combining several steps in one fast action. In this chapter we present several projects with practical appeal that are also perfect for gift-giving, be it for your favorite gardener, creative cook, intrepid traveler, or boating buddy. They allow you to combine standard machine sewing and serging techniques, or they can be easily adapted for machine sewing.

The Basics

Don't for a moment think that you must have a serger to make the projects we feature in this chapter. Adapt the patterns to the traditional sewing machine techniques you are used to. If you have a serger or are thinking of getting one, you'll find helpful information and a collection of projects tailor-made for serging.

Tools and Materials

If you'll be using a serger to make the projects in this chapter, there are a few specialized items and tips you should know to make your work progress more smoothly.

SERGER

A serger, also known as an overlock machine, is a sewing machine that sews, finishes, and trims in one step—at a speed of up to 1,500 stitches per minute. It duplicates the professional seam finishes usually found in manufactured goods and allows you to create decorative edgings and effects. A serger will not replace a traditional sewing machine, but it will be an adjunct to it, saving you sewing time.

Sergers use two, three, four, or five threads and one or two needles to create stitches. You can achieve an array of stitches and finishes on a variety of fabrics with an interesting selection of threads. A blade trims the edge of the fabric to a predetermined width, allowing the stitches to encase the raw edge.

Test threads, stitches, and tension on scrap fabric before beginning any sewing. With almost any project, you will find some way to incorporate a serger into your regular sewing process.

NEEDLES AND PINS

Follow your machine manual to find the needles suited to the thread and fabric weight you are working with. For four-thread stitches, you will need two needles. When working with one needle, remove the needle that is not being used. Using either the left or the right needle on a two-needle serger will give you the option of varying the stitch width.

Use long straight pins with plastic heads for clear visibility. Unlike a sewing machine, a serger cannot stitch over pins because of the cutting knives. Take care to remove all pins before they reach the knife.

THREAD

All threads can be used on a serger. Choose strong, quality thread—weak thread may break when a serger is sewing at very high speeds. Use 100 percent cotton, 100 percent polyester, cotton-wrapped polyester, or nylon for general serging. For decorative stitching, choose rayon, metallics, silk, or buttonhole twist. For heavier coverage, use woolly nylon or a thicker thread, such as perlé cotton or a lightweight yarn.

Woolly thread is also available with a metallic finish. For thread that blends with any color fabric, use invisible nylon. Use heavy threads only in the loopers, as they have holes large enough to accommodate thick thread. Test and adjust tension whenever you change threads.

Use a pressing cloth and medium heat when pressing over any decorative threads, especially those containing nylon.

MARKING

Use a disappearing marker and make any markings on the seamline longer, so they will not be trimmed away or covered with stitching. Pretest all markers on a fabric scrap before using.

CUTTING

Use the same cutting tools as for regular sewing, including dressmaking shears, embroidery scissors, or craft snips, and a rotary cutter and cutting mat. Most sergers are equipped with a cutter for breaking thread ends. If you need to rip serged seams, use a surgical seam ripper with a sharp, hooked blade.

Fabric

Any fabric, from heavyweight denims to fine silks and cottons, can be serged. Test the tension on a scrap of fabric before beginning, and make any adjustments necessary. Try to sew at a constant speed to maintain even stitch quality, especially on heavy fabrics or when stitching through several layers. Consult your serger manual for information on fabrics and stitches.

Accessories

Most sergers include a package of the basic tools you will need for serger sewing. These usually include long-armed tweezers, which are essential in the threading process, spool holders, thread nets, and looper threaders. If your serger does not come with a threader, either purchase one separately or use a dental floss threader. Other useful items include self-adhesive seam allowance decal, a needle gripper, liquid stabilizer, and seam sealant.

PERFORMING FEET

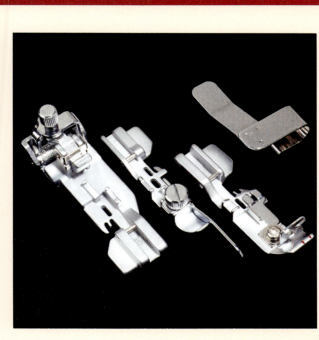

There are several feet and attachments that will help you get the most out of your serger. They are listed below in the order in which they appear in the photo, viewed left to right.

ELASTICATOR FOOT stretches elastic as it is being stitched onto fabric.

BLINDSTITCH FOOT maintains even stitch width for blind hemming and sewing along folds.

CORDING FOOT has a groove in the front that allows cord to be threaded through and stitched over for embellishment.

GATHERING ATTACHMENT allows fabric to be gathered and stitched in one step, or one piece of fabric can be gathered and stitched to a second piece.

THREAD ENDS

TIPS FOR FINISHING

There are several methods for finishing the stitching at the beginning and end of seams. Sometimes ends will be serged over with another row of stitching to secure them. Other methods include weaving in the ends or using seam sealant, as below. Experiment to find the best method for your project.

Weave in the ends. Slide a crochet hook, bodkin, or loop turner under the last 1¹/2" (3.8 cm) of stitching. Catch the thread chain with the hook and pull it through. Trim any remaining thread. Alternately, thread the chain through a tapestry needle or bodkin and weave it through the stitching for 1¹/2" (3.8 cm). Trim any excess.

Apply Seam Sealant. Knot the thread ends close to the edge of the fabric and trim close to the knot. Apply a seam sealant, such as Fray Check®, a clear liquid that will prevent the ends from fraying and knots from untying. Follow manufacturer's instructions and test on scrap fabric first.

Special Stitches

Serger stitches are made either with two, three, four, or five threads. Length and width can be adjusted according to the end use of the stitch and the fabric.

The rolled hem capability of your serger will allow you to serge even the most delicate fabrics, such as those used in heirloom sewing. Some of the heirloom projects in Chapter 2 of this book can be adapted for use with a serger.

Rolled Hem. This is a narrow short stitch that causes the edge of the fabric to roll slightly to the wrong side. Use a two- or three-thread stitch, and if desired, use a decorative thread and short stitch length for a corded look. Consult your manual for any necessary adjustments—you may need to adjust the needle plate or presser foot.

Decorative Edging. Use a regular overlock stitch and shorten the stitch length. Closer stitches will give the appearance of satin stitching. When using woolly nylon, the fibers will separate to fill the space between the stitches, creating a denser edging.

Trims

A serger permits you to make your own braid trim to enhance clothing, placemats and napkins, and a variety of other projects. Use topstitching thread in the upper looper and make decorative overlock stitches on top of 1/8" (3 mm) wide ribbon. Use the single strip as a trim or braid several strips together for a unique look with depth. You can also overlock over cords, rickrack, or yarns to make interesting trims or braids. Use your creativity to invent new trim ideas.

Making Tubes

Serger-made tubes come in handy for a number of uses. They can be fashioned into handles for bags and totes, used as ties and belts for dolls and toys, or several colors can be braided together for an attractive trim.

Cut narrow strips of fabric 3/4" (2 cm) wide and the desired length. Run a chain of stitches the length of the strip plus 2" (5 cm). Do not cut the chain. Place the fabric right side up, pull the thread chain forward and lay it lengthwise down the center, leaving a 2" (5 cm) tail at the bottom.

Fold the strip in half, right sides together; keep the thread chain at the fold and overlock the raw edges together. Cut the thread from the machine and remove the tube. Gently pull on the 2" (5 cm) thread tail and the fabric will turn itself inside out.

Using a Serger For Craft Sewing

Serger use need not be confined to the crafts we show you here. Your ingenuity and sewing know-how will help you adapt other craft sewing projects for serger sewing. Even heirloom projects, such as the christening gown (page 46), can have laces stitched together and construction seams sewn with a serger. Try making serged pin tucks: Fold the fabric along the line of the tuck and sew along the edge with a narrow stitch. For heirloom sewing, use a narrow rolled-edge stitch with a short stitch length and fine thread. The initial seam in a French seam can also be made on a serger. Small quilting projects can also be stitched with a serger, which will produce a consistent seam allowance.

Gifts for the Gardener

W hat weekend gardener could resist this collection of colorful gardening gear? The apron and mat add a level of comfort to the task, while the bucket pockets hold all the necessities. Green thumb not included.

SIZE

Apron is 29" x 30" (73.5 cm x 76 cm); kneeling mat is 12¹/₄" x 18¹/₂" (31 cm x 47 cm); bucket pocket is 9" x 14" (23 cm x 35.5 cm)

MATERIALS

Note: Materials and instructions are for the 3 items.

- 1¹/₄ yds. (1.15 m) toile print medium-weight fabric
- ¹/₂ yd. (.5 m) coordinating striped medium-weight fabric
- Paper-backed fusible web
- ¹/₂ yd. (.5 m) heavy-gauge plastic
- High-loft quilt batting
- 3 yds. (2.75 m) matching ribbon ⁷/₈" (2 mm) wide
- 13" (33 cm) piece of Velcro®
- 48" (122 cm) cording
- Matching threads and 1 spool woolly nylon
- Disappearing marker
- Hot-glue gun and glue sticks
- 2¹/₂-gallon (10 l) plastic bucket
- Serger and sewing machine with zipper foot

CUTTING

Toile fabric

Cut 29¹/₂" x 30¹/₂" (75 cm x 77.5 cm) piece for apron.

Cut 9¹/₄" x 13¹/₂" (23.5 cm x 34 cm) apron pocket (match pattern placement on apron, if desired).

Cut 2 pieces each 9¹/₂" x 14¹/₂" (24 cm x 37 cm) for bucket pocket backs.

Cut 2 bias strips each 1¹/₂" x 12" (3.8 cm x 30.5 cm) for mat handles.

Striped fabric

Cut 2 pieces each 6¹/₂" x 22¹/₂" (16.5 cm x 57 cm) for bucket pockets.

Cut 2 pieces each 12¹/₂" x 18¹/₂" (32 cm x 47 cm) for mat.

Paper-backed fusible web

Cut 2 pieces each 9¹/₂" x 14¹/₂" (24 cm x 37 cm) for bucket pocket back.

Cut 2 pieces each 6¹/₂" x 22¹/₂" (16.5 cm x 57 cm) for bucket pockets.

Batting

Cut 2 pieces each 12¹/₂" x 18¹/₂" (32 cm x 47 cm).

APRON

Following cutting diagram (page 132), mark apron outlines on wrong side of apron fabric. Cut out. On right side, mark pocket placement. Fold pocket in half crosswise and mark vertical center. Serge around all edges of pocket. Matching markings, stitch pocket to apron with sewing machine along side and lower edges. Stitch along marked center of pocket. Serge around remaining edges of apron. Cut a 20" (51 cm) length of ribbon for neck strap. Cut remaining ribbon in half for waist ties. Stitch ribbons in place with sewing machine.

KNEELING MAT

Layer mat pieces from bottom to top as follows: striped fabric with wrong side up, 2 layers of batting, striped fabric with right side up, plastic. Baste all layers together with sewing machine and ¹/₄" (6 mm) seam allowance. Serge around all edges to finish.

To make handles, cut cording in half. Matching top edge of cord and fabric, fold fabric strip around cord, so that wrong side faces out. With zipper foot, stitch fabric close to cord, then across end, through center of cord. Starting at top, push fabric along cord to turn to right side as shown. Trim remaining cord and knot ends of handles. With zipper foot, stitch to each end of mat with zipper foot.

BUCKET POCKETS

Following manufacturer's instructions, fuse paper-backed fusible web to wrong side of 1 pocket back. Remove paper backing. Peel VELCRO® apart. Stitch hook side of VELCRO® to wrong side of fused fabric 3/4" (2 cm) below top edge. Fuse remaining background fabric to wrong side of remaining piece. With marker, mark lower edge of right side at 3 1/2" (9 cm) intervals. Mark 1/2" (1.3 cm) in from each edge, and 1/2" (1.3 cm) to either side of marked intervals.

Fuse striped pocket fabrics together. Mark along lower edge at 5 1/2" (14 cm) intervals. With woolly nylon in upper looper and matching thread in lower looper and needle, and following serger manual, set serger for 3-thread closely spaced overlock stitch. Serge top edge of pocket.

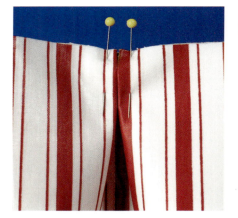

After stitching pockets in place, make pocket pleats, fold fabric at 1/2" (1.3 cm) markings to stitching lines and pin in place. With sewing machine, baste pocket pleats in place 1/8" (3 mm) from lower edges. Serge around all edges to finish, covering stitching lines on sides and lower edge.

With sewing machine and matching thread at side and lower edges, stitch pocket to background fabric with raw edges even. Matching markings on pocket and 3 1/2" (9 cm) markings on background, stitch pockets in place from lower edge to top serged edge.

Place pocket against bucket to mark placement. Hot-glue loop side of VELCRO® to bucket. Press pocket in place.

TIP

Choose fabric treated with Scotchguard® or spray on a stain-resistant finish to repel water and dirt.

Beat-the-Heat Hotpads

Delight yourself or a favorite cook with matching oven mitt, pot holder, coasters, and potpourri scented trivet. With Teflon-coated fabric and fleece lining this set can take on any items too hot to handle.

SIZE

Trivet is 9" (23 cm) square; pot holder is 9" (23 cm) square; oven mitt is 6¹/₂" x 11¹/₂" (16.5 cm x 29 cm); coasters are 4¹/₂" (11.5 cm) square

MATERIALS

Note: Materials and instructions are for 1 each of trivet, pot holder, oven mitt, and 3 coasters.

- ¹/₄ yd. (.25 m) each of plaid, striped and print heavy-weight cotton fabrics
- ¹/₄ yd. (.25 m) quilted Teflon-coated fabric
- ¹/₄ yd. (.25 m) muslin
- ¹/₄ yd. (.25 m) fleece
- 2 spools decorative thread
- 3 spools matching thread
- Cinnamon sticks and potpourri
- Serger and sewing machine

CUTTING

Note: Patterns are on pages 132-133.

Trivet

Cut a 9" (23 cm) square each from striped and plaid fabrics.

Cut 2 squares each 9" (23 cm) from muslin.

Cut a 9" (23 cm) square each from fleece and Teflon fabric.

Pot holder

Cut a 7" (18 cm) square from print fabrics.

Cut 2 squares each 5" (12.5 cm) from striped fabric, so stripes run diagonally. Cut squares in half diagonally across stripes to make 4 triangles.

Cut a 9" (23 cm) square each from fleece and Teflon fabric.

Cut a 1¹/₂" x 5" (4 cm x 12.5 cm) tab from print.

Oven mitt

Cut 2 of pattern A from plaid fabric.

Cut pattern B from Teflon fabric.
Cut 2 of pattern C from print.
Cut pattern C from fleece.
Cut a 1¹/₂" x 5" (4 cm x 12.5 cm) tab from print fabric.

Coasters

Cut 6 squares each 4¹/₂" (11.5 cm) from assorted fabrics.

Cut 3 squares each 4¹/₂" (11.5 cm) from fleece.

SERGER SETUP

Following serger manual, set serger for left needle construction. For decorative edges, place decorative thread in both loopers.

TRIVET

Serge along one edge of Teflon square to finish opening. Place striped and plaid squares with wrong sides together, then place fleece between. Serge along one edge to finish opening. Place striped side on wrong side of Teflon fabric and serge around remaining 3 sides.

Place muslin squares together and serge around 3 sides. Lightly fill pocket with cinnamon and potpourri and serge remaining side closed. Slip filling inside trivet.

POT HOLDER

Place long sides of triangles on each side of square with right sides together. Serge seams. Press seams open to make large square. Place pieced square and Teflon fabric with wrong sides together, then place fleece between.

To make tab, make a 6" (15 cm) chain on serger. Fold tab strip in half lengthwise with right sides together and place chain inside fold. Serge across one short edge and long raw edge. Pull chain to turn strip to right side. Press. Pin tab in place on short straight edge and serge edge, catching tab in stitching.

OVEN MITT

Following pattern piece letters, place C pieces together with wrong sides facing. Place fleece C between them and serge along straight edge. With wrong sides together, match curved edges of B and C pieces. Serge edges together.

To make tab, make a 6" (15 cm) chain on serger. Fold tab strip in half lengthwise with right sides together and place chain inside fold. Serge across one short edge and long raw edge.

Pull chain to turn strip to right side. Press. Place 2 A pieces with wrong sides together. Place tab on one edge and serge around all 4 edges, catching tab in stitching.

Fold lower edge of B piece up to match top edge of A piece and serge together around sides.

COASTERS

Place fleece between pairs of fabric squares. Serge around all edges.

FINISHING

Weave in or finish ends as desired (see Thread Ends, page 84).

TIPS

- Take care when choosing decorative threads. Do not use nylon, as it will melt when exposed to extreme heat. Use cotton or rayon thread or fine wool yarn; do not use metallics.
- Use quilt patterns as inspiration for potholder designs. You can also use pieced designs to make trivet tops. Vary coasters by joining 2 triangles of contrasting fabrics to make a square.

Breezy Wind Socks

From the porch, from a flagpole, from your yacht—these flashy wind socks make an impressive sight with their streamers blowing in the breeze. Ours are made from cotton, but rip-stop nylon can also be used.

SIZE

Wind socks are 42$^{1}/_{2}$" (108 cm) long and 7$^{1}/_{2}$" (19 cm) in diameter; streamers are 28$^{1}/_{2}$" (72 cm) long

MATERIALS

Each Wind Sock
- 2 yds. (1.85 m) nylon cording
- $^{3}/_{4}$ yd. (.70 m) nylon boning
- Plastic ring $^{3}/_{4}$" (2 cm) in diameter
- Pressing cloth
- Large-eyed darning needle
- Serger and sewing machine

Sun and Moon Wind Sock
- 1$^{1}/_{4}$ yd. (1.15 m) orange fabric
- $^{1}/_{4}$ yd. (.25 m) blue fabric
- 9" x 19" (23 cm x 48 cm) piece yellow fabric
- 11" x 12" (28 cm x 30.5 cm) piece white fabric
- 1$^{3}/_{8}$ yds. (1.3 m) paper-backed fusible web
- Red thread and woolly nylon
- Red fabric paint

Seashell Wind Sock
- 1$^{1}/_{4}$ yd (1.15 m) blue-green fabric
- 11" x 26" (28 cm x 66 cm) piece yellow fabric
- 13" x 20" (33 cm x 51 cm) piece white fabric
- 1 yd. (1 m) paper-backed fusible web
- White thread and woolly nylon
- Aqua fabric paint

CUTTING

Note: Patterns are on pages 133-134.

Sun and Moon Wind Sock
Orange fabric
  Cut a 16" x 23$^{3}/_{4}$" (40.5 cm x 60.5 cm) body.
  Cut 8 streamers each 3$^{3}/_{4}$" x 30$^{1}/_{2}$" (9.5 cm x 77.5 cm).

Paper-backed fusible web
  Cut a 5" x 40" (12.5 cm x 101.5 cm) piece for background blocks.
  Cut a 9" x 19" (23 cm x 48 cm) piece for suns and stars.
  Cut a 11" x 12" (28 cm x 30.5 cm) piece for moons.

Seashell Wind Sock
Blue-green fabric
  Cut a 16" x 23$^{3}/_{4}$" (40.5 cm x 60.5 cm) body.
  Cut 8 streamers each 3$^{3}/_{4}$" x 30$^{1}/_{2}$" (9.5 cm x 77.5 cm).

Yellow fabric
  Cut a 3$^{1}/_{2}$" x 23$^{3}/_{4}$" (9 cm x 60.5 cm) strip for upper band.
  Cut a 3" x 23$^{3}/_{4}$" (7.5 cm x 60.5 cm) strip for middle band.
  Cut a 1$^{3}/_{4}$" x 23$^{3}/_{4}$" (4.5 cm x 60.5 cm) strip for lower band.

Paper-backed fusible web
  Cut a 3$^{1}/_{2}$" x 23$^{3}/_{4}$" (9 cm x 60.5 cm) strip for upper band.
  Cut a 3" x 23$^{3}/_{4}$" (7.5 cm x 60.5 cm) strip for middle band.
  Cut a 1$^{3}/_{4}$" x 23$^{3}/_{4}$" (4.5 cm x 60.5 cm) strip for lower band.

Note: If using nylon fabric, zigzag appliqués in place. Test fusibles first with a pressing cloth and medium heat. Test fabric paint before using to see that it adheres well. If necessary, use machine embroidery and colored thread instead.

SUN AND MOON WIND SOCK

Draw 8 blocks each 5" (12.5 cm) square onto paper side of fusible web. Following manufacturer's instructions, fuse to wrong side of blue fabric and cut out. Trace 4 moons onto fusible web and fuse to white fabric. Trace 4 each of suns and stars to remaining fusible web and fuse to yellow fabric. Cut out all shapes. Lightly trace circles onto suns.

Lay orange body fabric lengthwise onto work surface. Position blocks onto fabric, 2" (5 cm) above lower edge, 3/4" (2 cm) in from each side and 3/4" (2 cm) apart. Fuse in place. Fuse moons and stars to alternate blocks, suns to remaining blocks. Paint over marked lines with red paint.

STREAMERS

With woolly nylon in upper looper and thread in lower looper and both needles, following serger manual, set machine for overlock stitch. Serge both long edges and one end of each streamer, trimming 1/2" (1.3 cm). With right sides together, pin streamers to lower edge of body, 1/4" (6 mm) from each end and next to each other. With serger, stitch streamers in place, trimming 1/4" (6 mm) from edges. Turn seam allowance toward body and press in place. **Note:** Use pressing cloth and medium heat to press woolly nylon.

SEASHELL WIND SOCK

Trace 3 each of small shells and large shells onto 13" x 20" (33 cm x 51 cm) piece of fusible web. Following manufacturer's instructions, fuse web to wrong side of white fabric. Cut out around marked outlines. With pencil, lightly trace shell markings onto shells.

Draw a wave pattern onto one long edge of fusible web for upper and lower bands, and onto both long edges for middle band. Continue waves along entire length of strips. Fuse web to wrong sides of yellow fabric strips and cut out.

Fuse lower yellow band onto

one long edge of blue-green body fabric. Center middle band 5 1/2" (14 cm) above lower edge. Fuse upper band in place along upper edge. Center one large shell on body 2 3/4" (7 cm) above lower edge. Place remaining shells 1 1/2" (3.8 cm) to either side. Fuse large shells in place.

Center 2 small shells between large shells in upper blue-green band. Cut 1 small shell in half lengthwise and place halves on each side, 1/4" (6 mm) from side edges. Fuse small shells and shell halves in place. Paint over pencil lines with aqua paint.

TIPS

- Use a lightweight fusible to add appliqués, and choose the lightest weight fabrics you can find for the body of the wind sock.
- If you want your wind sock to be weather-resistant and have a long life, rip-stop nylon and nylon taffeta are good fabric choices.
- Choose your own designs to appliqué. Be inspired by the seasons or special holidays, or make a wind sock to announce special events, such as the birth of a baby.

CASING

Press top edge 2¹/₂" (6.5 cm) to wrong side, then press 1¹/₄" (3 cm) to right side to make accordion fold as shown. Pin in place. Serge along edge through all layers. Turn to right side and press flat. Insert boning into casing. Trim boning ¹/₂" less than width of top edge. With right sides together, serge side seam, keeping needle clear of boning.

ATTACHING CORDS

Divide casing into 3 equal parts and mark. Cut 3 cords each 20" (51 cm) long. Thread cord into darning needle and knot one end. Pass needle through casing at marking and below boning. Thread needle through ring, then back through casing beside first stitch. Remove needle and knot end. Repeat at remaining 2 markings. Knot 8" (20.5 cm) piece of cord through ring for hanger.

Dressed-Up Basket

A tisket, a tasket, you can dress up any basket! The technique for making this simple ruffled liner can be adapted to fit most baskets. This base is a separate piece that can be glued in place or left loose for easy laundering.

SIZE

Liner fits a 9" (23 cm) diameter basket with sides 4" (10 cm) high

MATERIALS

- ■ 1/2 yd. (.5 m) cotton print fabric
- ■ 3/4 yd. (.7 m) elastic 1/4" (6 mm) wide
- ■ Rayon machine-embroidery thread in contrasting color
- ■ Matching thread
- ■ Elasticator foot for serger
- ■ Gathering foot for serger
- ■ Circle of quilt batting 7" (18 cm) in diameter
- ■ Basket 9" (23 cm) in diameter
- ■ Serger and sewing machine
- ■ Hot-glue gun and glue sticks, if desired

CUTTING

Print fabric

Cut a 4" x 45" (10 cm x 115 cm) ruffle strip.

Cut 12" x 45" (30.5 cm x 115 cm) liner.

Cut 2 circles 7" (18 cm) in diameter for base.

BASE

Place base circles with right sides together; place batting on bottom. With sewing machine, stitch together with 1/4" (6 mm) seam, leaving a 2" (5 cm) opening for turning. Clip seams evenly around and turn right side out. Press seam allowance to inside and slipstitch opening closed.

RUFFLE

Press ruffle strip in half lengthwise. With decorative thread in upper looper, sewing thread in lower looper and needle, and with a stitch length of 2, following serger manual, set serger for rolled hem. Roll-hem the folded edge, trimming 1/8" (3 mm) from the edge with serger blade.

LINER

Press liner in half. Following serger manual, attach elasticator. With three-thread overlock stitch and matching raw edges of ruffle and liner, serge elastic to liner and ruffle, gathering at a 2 to 1 ratio and trimming 1/4" (6 mm) from edges.

Following serger manual, attach gathering foot. With four-thread stitch and machine set for differential feed of 2, gather folded edge of liner, trimming 3/8" (1 cm) from edges.

With right sides together, serge short ends of liner, matching rolled hem edges and gathered edges, and trimming 1" (2.5 cm) from edges.

FINISHING

Place liner in basket with ruffle over basket edge. Adjust gathers. Place base inside basket. Base may be hot-glued in place, if desired, or left loose for easy laundering.

Gent's Garment Bag

For the traveling man who deserves a distinctive gift, this garment bag is a standout. Vary the fabric for a more feminine version. The zipper, which is bought by the yard, is easily serged in place.

SIZE

Garment bag is 22" x 48¹/₂"
(56 cm x 123.5 cm)

MATERIALS

- 1¹/₂ yds. (1.4 m) medium-weight fabric
- 1³/₈ yds. (1.3 m) zipper (purchased by the yd. (m)) with 2 zipper pulls
- ¹/₄ yd. (.25 m) navy grosgrain ribbon ¹/₄" (6 mm) wide

- Wooden coat hanger
- Thread and woolly nylon in matching color

CUTTING

Cut a 22¹/₂" x 50" (57 cm x 127 cm) bag back.
Cut 2 bag fronts each 11¹/₂" x 50" (29 cm x 127 cm).
Cut 2 handles each 3" x 14¹/₂" (7.5 cm x 36.5 cm).
Cut a 2¹/₂" x 3" (6.5 cm x 7.5 cm) piece for zipper guard.

ZIPPER

Following serger manual, thread upper looper with woolly nylon, lower looper and right needle with matching thread. With 1" (2.5 cm) of zipper extending off upper and lower edges of bag front, place zipper tape and one front together with right sides facing. Pin zipper in place. Stitching on wrong side of zipper, serge zipper to fabric, close to zipper teeth and trimming zipper tape and fabric. Fold zipper back and press on the right side. Do not let iron come in contact with woolly nylon.

Place remaining bag front against opposite side of zipper and stitch. Place zipper pulls on each end.

Serge around edges of zipper guard. With raw edges even, fold lengthwise into thirds and pin in place at top of zipper as shown. With sewing machine, stitch in place along top edge of guard. Fold guard up, turning last third to wrong side of front and stitch in place from front through all layers. Satin-stitch bar tacks 1" (2.5 cm) from top of bag through zipper.

BAG

Place front and back with right sides together. Lay coat hanger on bag at zipper guard and trace top shape. Curve center top for hanger opening. Round off lower corners. Serge around hanger opening.

HANDLES

Press handles in half with right sides together. Open. Press side edges to center fold, then press along fold again. Stitch along both edges with sewing machine.

ASSEMBLY

Pin handles to front of bag, 2¹/₄" (5.5 cm) on either side of center front. *Open zipper partway.* With right sides together, serge bag front and back together, stitching over handles. Turn bag right side out and press. Cut ribbon in half. Thread a piece through each zipper pull, tie in a knot and trim ends.

On-the-Go Lunch Bag

Brown-bagging it never looked so appealing as when lunch is toted in a reusable sack made especially to turn an ordinary routine into a festive meal. Laminated fabric allows for easy cleanup.

SIZE

Lunch bag is 7½" x 14" x 4½" (19 cm x 35.5 cm x 11.5 cm)

MATERIALS

- ½ yd. (.5 m) laminated fabric 45" (115 cm) wide
- Matching or contrasting threads
- Seam sealant
- Disappearing marker
- 1" (2.5 cm) piece VELCRO®
- Serger and sewing machine

CUTTING

Cut out lunch bag in one piece following cutting diagram (page 134). Transfer all pattern markings to fabric.

With wrong sides together, stitch lines C, D, and E from upper to lower edges. Stitch along top edge. With right sides together, stitch remaining sides. On outside, overlock stitched seam.

SIDES

Set serger for a narrow three-thread overlock stitch following serger manual. Following letters on cutting diagram (page 134), and with right sides together, fold along line A. Stitch along line to large dot. Serge off edge of fabric. Tie a knot in ends close to dot. Repeat for B.

BASE

Place front and back lower straight edges with right sides facing. Stitch. With right sides together, bring point at end of A to end of lower edge seam to make a V. Stitch both sides of V for side base seam. Repeat for other side.

FINISHING

Finish all seams with seam sealant, following manufacturer's instructions. Turn bag right side out. Fold over top edges twice and place 2 markings for VELCRO® placement. Stitch VELCRO® in place at markings.

CHAPTER 5

From Your Scrap Basket

We who love to sew and craft with fabric usually can't bear to part with the bits and pieces that are left over when a project is completed. These invariably go into a collection of odds and ends from other projects past. Inside every scrap bag or basket are the makings of countless new projects just waiting to be conceived. With a diversity of sewings techniques, such as appliqué and piecing, and the marvel of fusibles, there's very little your imagination can dream up that can't be made from scraps. You'll probably find a few new ideas in this chapter. You'll certainly find the inspiration.

The Basics

Recycling bits and pieces of fabric from finished projects into a new craft creation illustrates the crafter's creed that nothing goes to waste. Scrapcraft lends itself beautifully to techniques that employ fusibles. This section offers suggestions for projects in addition to those in this chapter.

Tools of the Trade

The uses for leftover fabric pieces are endless. All you need are imagination, skill, and general sewing supplies. Look at the tools in the previous chapters to meet specific technique needs.

CUTTING

Sharp, good quality scissors, embroidery scissors or craft snips, and a rotary cutter and self-healing cutting mat will cater to most of your general crafting needs. Pinking shears or a rotary cutter with a pinking blade are helpful for making decorative edgings.

MEASURING

Tape measure, acrylic rulers, and templates in a variety of shapes will make measuring and marking easier.

MARKING

Use lead pencil, tailor's chalk, dressmaker's carbon paper and wheel, and disappearing markers, depending on the requirements of the project.

NEEDLES AND PINS

Have a variety of needles on hand for hand sewing and embroidery, as well as straight pins and safety pins.

THREADS

Sewing threads in a variety of colors and decorative threads, such as metallics, silk, or rayon machine-embroidery thread, will suit most purposes. Invisible nylon thread blends with any fabric. Embroidery floss and perlé cotton are useful for hand embellishing.

SEWING MACHINE AND SERGER

A machine with decorative stitching capability offers many design possibilities. Using a serger for seams and decorative edges will save sewing time.

GLUES

White craft glue or fabric glue work well for gluing fabrics to surfaces that can't be stitched through. A hot-glue gun and glue sticks are helpful when a fast-drying, strong bond is required. Temporary glues allow appliqués and trims to be removed before laundering.

FABULOUS FUSIBLES

The introduction of fusible products for the craft sewer has widened creative possibilities and made available new time-saving techniques. For best results, follow manufacturer's instructions for all products. Use a pressing cloth and a barrier, such as a piece of paper, on the ironing board to protect the surfaces of the iron and board.

FUSIBLE WEB. Available alone or with a paper backing. Allows two fabrics to be joined together, or fabric to be adhered to cardboard or any surface that will accept heat. Paper-backed will turn any fabric into an iron-on. Simply iron the web to the wrong side of the fabric, cut out the shape, then remove the paper backing. Place the motif in position and iron in place.

FUSIBLE TAPE. Works in the same manner as fusible web, and its narrow width makes it useful for hemming and fusing ribbons and trims in place.

FUSIBLE INTERFACING. Adds body and drape to lightweight fabrics.

FUSIBLE FLEECE. Is a time-saving alternative to batting in small quilting projects that don't require quilting stitches to be worked over them. It can also be used as an embellishment (see the Advent Wall Hanging, page 114).

FUSIBLE THREAD. Use fusible thread to stitch around an appliqué shape, just inside the seamline. Clip seam allowance as necessary, then turn the seam allowance to the wrong side and press to the backing fabric. The fusible thread will secure the seam allowance in place while appliqué is being stitched.

FABRIC AND TRIMS

Almost any size fabric scrap can be utilized in a project. The first step in sorting fabrics is to divide those in your scrap basket by type. Combine fabrics of similar weight and requiring similar care. The next step is to decide on a color scheme. Since the pieces in your scrap basket probably reflect some of your favorite colors, choosing those that work well together shouldn't be too difficult. Look through your leftover trims for bits of lace, rickrack, ribbon, and braid that can be recycled. Odd buttons, beads, and even unwanted costume jewelry can become stunning embellishments when added to a scrap project.

PROJECT IDEAS

• Use the lunch bag instructions on page 100 to make gift bags, adjusting the size to fit the gift.

• Recycle fabrics into gift bags that the receivers can use again. Use patchwork techniques to make the bags or use a single fabric and fuse appliqués to it.

• Use assorted fabrics to line baskets that can be filled with goodies. Adapt the instructions on page 97 to fit your own baskets.

• With decorative thread, serge or zigzag florist's wire to the edge of fabric strips to make wire-edged ribbon for crafting.

• Trim scraps into squares with pinking shears. Push them at their centers into a foam wreath base or into a foam ball until it is completely covered. Attach ribbon and hang.

• Use fabric leftovers to make most of the projects in this book. Try the pot holders, the teddy bear, the photo frame, even the quilts. Projects take on a character of their own when they are made with a collection of fabric remnants.

Clowning Around

Cute-as-can-be clowns can be used to embellish any number of projects—as here, where they join hands around a sewing basket and dangle from the ribbon tied to the scissors. They are also a sweet favor just by themselves.

SIZE

Clowns are 5$\frac{1}{2}$" (14 cm) tall

MATERIALS

Note: Materials and instructions are for one scissor clown and 4 basket clowns.

- Remnants of assorted red, white, and blue cotton print fabrics
- 4" x 6" (10 cm x 15 cm) piece of blue cotton fabric
- 4" x 6" (10 cm x 15 cm) piece of blue gingham cotton fabric
- 12" (30.5 cm) square of white felt
- 1$\frac{1}{4}$ yds. (1.15 m) white lace $\frac{1}{4}$" (6 mm) wide ($\frac{1}{4}$ yd./.25 m per doll)
- 2$\frac{1}{2}$ yds. (2.3 m) red satin ribbon $\frac{1}{8}$" (3 mm) wide ($\frac{1}{2}$ yd./.5 m per doll)
- $\frac{1}{2}$ yd. (.5 m) red embossed satin ribbon $\frac{3}{8}$" (10 mm) wide
- Polyester fiberfill
- 5 wooden beads $\frac{3}{4}$" (20 mm) in diameter
- 5 small white pom-poms
- 10 small red or white buttons
- Wicker basket, 5$\frac{1}{2}$" x 6$\frac{1}{2}$" x 3" (14 cm x 16.5 cm x 7.5 cm)
- White acrylic paint and paint-brush
- Embroidery scissors
- White craft glue
- Hot-glue gun and glue sticks
- Needle and white thread
- Fine-tip black and pink markers
- Cardboard

CUTTING

Note: Patterns on page 135 include $\frac{1}{4}$" (6 mm) seam allowance.

White and blue prints
Cut 5 clown bodies from each.

Red print
Cut 5 hats.

White felt
Cut 5 collars.

HEAD

With black markers, mark eyes, lashes, and mouth. Make star cheeks with pink marker. Fold hat piece in half lengthwise with right sides together. Stitch side seam and turn right side out. Press $\frac{1}{4}$" (6 mm) to wrong side along raw edge and glue in place. Glue pom-pom to tip of hat. Glue hat to head.

BODY

With right sides together, stitch white and blue body pieces together along center with a $\frac{1}{4}$" (6 mm) seam. Press seam open. Press $\frac{1}{4}$" (6 mm) to wrong side at wrists. At wrist and ankle hems, place lace on right side, close to fold and stitch in place.

At shoulders, fold body in half with right sides together. Stitch side seams from wrist to ankle. Open legs, press hem under at ankle and apply lace as for wrists. Stitch inner leg seam. Clip seam allowances at underarms and crotch and turn right side out through arm or leg opening.

Make short running stitches around wrists and ankles 1/4" (6 mm) above lace, gather fabric tightly along thread and secure. Before closing last ankle, stuff clown with fiberfill.

BASKET

Paint basket white. Cut a 2 1/2" x 4" (6.5 cm x 11.5 cm) piece of cardboard. Roll cardboard to a gentle curve. Trim to fit inside of basket. Glue gingham fabric to

ASSEMBLY

With hot-glue gun, glue head to center of collar. Fold collar over body and glue in place at neck, shoulders, front, and back. With red ribbon, tie bows at wrists and ankles to cover running stitches. Glue or sew buttons to center front.

one side, trim edges to 1/2" (1.3 cm) beyond cardboard and glue to wrong side. Hot-glue cardboard piece into one end of basket, curving to fit.

To make pin cushion, trace top opening between cardboard and basket onto cardboard. Cut out. Place small amount of fiberfill on cardboard. Cut blue fabric 1" (2.5 cm) larger than cardboard. Cover cardboard and fiberfill with fabric, gluing raw edges to wrong side. Hot-glue pin cushion to cardboard and basket edges.

FINISHING

Sew 4 clowns together at wrists to make a row. Adjust and glue or stitch the row of clowns around the outside of basket. Glue ankles together at base of basket. Sew remaining wrists and ankles together. Sew one end of wide red ribbon to back of remaining doll. Tie opposite end to scissors.

Strip-Pieced Purses

Patchwork takes many forms, one of which is easy strip piecing, using strips of fabric pieced together to create a new fabric. Here's a trio of pretty and practical pouches for toting, spare change, and eyeglasses.

SIZE

Bag is 5³/4" x 6¹/2" (14.5 cm x 16.5 cm); eyeglass case is 4" x 7¹/2" (10 cm x 19 cm); change purse is 3" x 4¹/2" (7.5 cm x 11 cm)

MATERIALS

Note: Materials and instructions are for a set of 3 purses.

- ¹/4 yd. (.25 m) each of 6 coordinating cotton print fabrics
- ¹/2 yd. (.5 m) muslin or matching cotton print for lining
- Fusible fleece
- Narrow double-fold bias binding in blue, white, and yellow
- 1¹/4 yd. (1.15 m) matching rayon cord
- VELCRO® dots
- Sunflower appliqué or motif
- 5 green shank buttons each ⁵/8"

(15 mm) in diameter
- 6 assorted flat buttons each ¹/2" (13 mm) in diameter
- Matching sewing thread
- Craft glue
- Patchwork foot

CUTTING

Muslin or lining fabric

Cut a 6" x 16" (15 cm x 40.5 cm) bag lining.

Cut a 4" x 18" (10 cm x 46 cm) eyeglass case lining.

Cut a 4" x 8" (10 cm x 20.5 cm) change purse lining.

Fusible fleece

Cut for all pieces same sizes as muslin linings.

Assorted fabrics

Cut fabrics into 1¹/2" (3.8 cm) wide strips as needed.

Fuse fleece to wrong side of muslin or lining fabric. Pin the first strip right side up onto one long side of fleece with edges even. Stitch ¹/4" (6 mm) from side edge, using the patchwork foot as a guide. Stitch along opposite side ¹/8" (3 mm) from strip edge. Pin second strip over first with right sides together. Stitch strips together with ¹/4" (6 mm) seam. Turn second strip to right side and press.

PIECING

Cut required strips following individual project instructions.

DESIGN OPTIONS

- Try other fabric combinations for a variety of looks. For evening use, make the pieces in scraps of velvet, silk, satins, moirés, or upholstery fabric. Trim with metallic braids, embossed ribbons, or antique buttons. Trim the bag with an elegant piece of antique costume jewelry.

- For day use, try denim, Ultrasuede®, men's ties, quilting cottons, or a rainbow of solid colors with contrasting colored trims.

- Use satin, velvet, or grosgrain ribbon, as an alternative to bias binding.

Continue adding strips, turning each strip back over the fleece and pressing as before until lining and fleece are covered.

With a pencil, and using a jar lid, coffee tin, etc., in correct size, mark curved outline onto right side of one end of pieced fabric. Cut out along marked line.

Sew bias binding to the short straight edge. To apply binding, open out bias and pin to wrong side edge, with raw edges even. Machine-stitch along the crease on the binding. Fold binding over raw edge to front and slipstitch in place.

Fold wrong sides of purse together to make pocket, following instructions for individual projects, below. Stitch sides together over existing stitching. Apply binding continuously to remaining raw edges. Turn in raw end $1/4$" (6 mm) and slipstitch in place.

Bag: Fold up 6" (15 cm) from straight end. Bind with blue bias binding.

Eyeglass case: Fold up 7" (18 cm) from straight end. Cut a 4" (10 cm) piece of white bias binding. Fold in half and stitch edges together. Pin to case 1" (2.5 cm) below finished straight edge. Cover raw ends with binding.

Change purse: Fold up 3" (7.5 cm) from straight end. Bind with yellow bias binding.

FINISHING

Sew VELCRO® dots in place under flap for closures. Using photo on page 109 as a guide, glue sunflower to bag front. Machine-stitch cord to sides. Sew buttons across eyeglass case binding strip as shown. Sew green buttons to coin purse.

TIPS

- For tips on using a rotary cutter, see On the Cutting Edge, page 14.
- To prevent rows from curving, stitch in alternate directions.
- For a quilted look, stitch diagonal quilting lines in both directions after piecing.

Heavenly Tree Trimmers

Use remnants of celestial fabrics and embellish them with machine appliqué and embroidery to make these striking holiday ornaments that don't have to wait until Christmas to be enjoyed.

SIZE

Ornaments are 5" (12.5 cm) in diameter

MATERIALS

Note: Materials and instructions are for one ornament only. Appliqué patterns are on pages 135-136.

- 6½" x 13" (16.5 cm x 33 cm) piece celestial print fabric
- 6½" (16.5 cm) square yellow print fabric
- 6½" (16.5 cm) square fusible fleece
- 6½" (16.5 cm) square tear-away stabilizer
- 6 circles each 5" (12.5 cm) in diameter of cardboard or template plastic
- ¾ yd. (.7 m) decorative cording
- No. 2 lead pencil
- Brown and yellow sewing thread
- Craft glue
- Tracing paper

APPLIQUÉS

Center yellow motif onto background fabric. Place stabilizer on wrong side of background fabric and pin all layers together. Machine-appliqué motif in place with satin stitch (narrow, closely spaced zigzag stitch). Work straight stitch along marked design lines. Tear away stabilizer.

FINISHING

Make templates by tracing celestial patterns (see pages 135-136) onto tracing paper and cutting out. Place template onto yellow fabric and trace around outline. Transfer design details to motif. Fuse fleece to wrong side of yellow print fabric. Cut out motif.

Glue appliqué to one side of plastic or cardboard circle, centering design. Trim fabric ½" (1.3 cm) from edge, turn to wrong side and glue in place. Cover remaining plastic or cardboard circle in same manner.

Glue circles together. Matching center of cord with lower center of ornament, glue cord in place around ornament. Tack cord ends together where they meet at top of ornament. Tie ends in a knot and trim.

Advent Wall Hanging

Deck the halls with a host of easily appliquéd holiday stockings. Stuff with little gifts and share the fun counting down the days to Christmas.

SIZE

Wall hanging is 35½" (90 cm) square

MATERIALS

- 1 yd. (1 m) red pin-dot cotton fabric
- 1 yd. (1 m) green pin-dot cotton fabric
- ½ yd. (.5 m) each of two red Christmas print cotton fabrics
- Remnants of assorted Christmas print cotton fabrics in red, green, and a small piece of tan
- 1 yd. (1 m) fusible fleece
- Fusible web
- Red rayon machine-embroidery thread
- Matching sewing thread
- Cardboard or plastic for templates

CUTTING

Note: Appliqué patterns on page 136 do not include seam allowance. Other pieces listed below include ¼" (6 mm) seam allowance where appropriate.

Red pin-dot

Cut 1 block 5¾" (14.5 cm) square.

Cut 37½" (95 cm) square for backing.

Green pin-dot

Cut 24 blocks each 5¾" (14.5 cm) square.

Christmas print 1

Cut 20 sashing strips each 1½" x 5¾" (3.8 cm x 14.5 cm) and 4 sashing strips each 1½" x 30¼" (3.8 cm x 77 cm).

Christmas print 2

Cut 2 border strips each 2¾" x 30¼" (7 cm x 77 cm) and 2 strips each 2¾" x 35¼" (7 cm x 89.5 cm).

Red remnants

Cut 24 pairs of stockings.

Green remnant

Cut 1 tree.

Tan remnant

Cut 1 tree trunk.

Fusible fleece

Cut 24 cuffs.

Fusible web

Cut 24 stockings, 1 tree, and 1 trunk.

APPLIQUE

Following manufacturer's instructions, fuse wrong sides of pairs of stockings together.

Pin a stocking to center of each green pin-dot square. With red rayon embroidery thread, satin-stitch (narrow, closely spaced zigzag) around outer edges of each stocking, leaving top edge unstitched for pocket.

With top edges aligned and following manufacturer's instructions, fuse cuffs to top of each stocking. Fuse tree to center of red square. Fuse trunk below tree. Satin-stitch around all raw edges.

ASSEMBLY

Arrange blocks into 5 rows of 5 blocks each, with tree block in lower right-hand corner. Join blocks into rows with short sashing strips between each block; join rows with long sashing strips. Stitch shorter border strips to sides of hanging, longer border strips to top and bottom.

FINISHING

Fuse fleece to wrong side of wall hanging. Lay wall hanging top over wrong side of backing. Baste layers together. Press raw edges of backing ¼" (6 mm) to wrong side. Turn pressed edges to front and slipstitch in place.

Appliquéd Towels

A quick way to dress up store-bought towels and give your bathroom an instant face-lift is to trim them with brightly colored appliqués and finish them off with contrasting odds and ends from your scrap basket.

SIZE

Appliqués are for hand towels

MATERIALS

Note: Appliqué patterns are on page 137.

All Towels
- Purchased hand towel
- Paper-backed fusible web

- Matching sewing threads
- Appliqué foot

Heart Towel
- ¹/₄ yd. (.25 m) pink cotton print fabric
- White baby rickrack

Scottie Towel
- Remnants of 4 red cotton print fabrics

- 1 yd. (1 m) white ribbon ¹/₈" (3 mm) wide
- 3 red heart buttons
- Red thread

Fish Towel
- ¹/₄ yd. (.25 m) fish print fabric
- 9 white buttons ¹/₄" (6 mm) in diameter
- Blue rickrack

HEART TOWEL

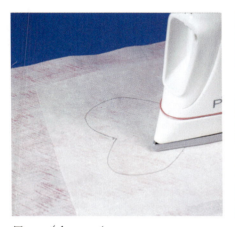

Trace 4 hearts (pattern on page 137) in a row onto paper side of fusible web. Cut out loosely around hearts, leaving a border of web. Following manufacturer's instructions, fuse web onto wrong side of fabric.

Cut out along marked outlines. Peel paper away from motifs. Space hearts evenly across woven band of towel. Fuse in place.

With appliqué foot, straight-stitch ¹/₈" (3 mm) inside edge of appliqué. Beginning at bottom of each heart, with straight stitch, stitch rickrack over stitching line.

SCOTTIE TOWEL

Trace 2 Scotties (pattern on page 137) and 2 reversed Scotties onto paper side of fusible web. Cut out loosely around each motif, leaving a border of web around the motif. Following manufacturer's instructions, fuse web onto wrong side of each fabric. Cut out along marked outlines. Peel paper away from motifs. Fuse in place. Space Scotties evenly across woven band of towel, facing the center. With appliqué foot, satin-stitch (narrow, closely spaced zigzag) around raw edges of Scotties. Cut ribbon into 4 equal lengths. Tie into bows and sew to necks of dogs. Sew buttons between dogs.

FISH TOWEL

Following manufacturer's instructions, fuse web onto wrong side of fabric. Cut out around individual fish. Peel paper away from motifs. Fuse fish as desired to one end of towel. With appliqué foot, satin-stitch (narrow, closely spaced zigzag) around raw edges of fish. Sew buttons around fish. Stitch rickrack along lower hem of towel.

Bouncing Baby Blocks

Little ones can learn letters and numbers and to identify shapes and animal faces from this set of fabric-covered appliquéd foam blocks—one of which even has pockets.

SIZE

Baby block is 5" (12.5 cm) square

MATERIALS

Note: Materials and instructions are for 4 blocks.

- $1/4$ yd. (.25 m) each of 6 assorted cotton print fabrics
- Paper-backed fusible web
- Fusible fleece
- Small amount of felt in a variety of colors
- 10" x 10" x 5" (25 cm x 25 cm x 12.5 cm) piece of high-density foam
- Pinking shears
- Disappearing marker
- Serrated-edge bread knife
- Sewing thread in matching colors
- Rayon machine-embroidery thread in matching colors
- Appliqué foot

CUTTING

Note: Appliqué patterns are on pages 137-140.

Assorted print fabrics

Cut each of 6 fabrics into 4 $5\frac{1}{2}$" (14 cm) squares.
  Cut 6 squares each 3" (7.5 cm).
  Cut 6 animal faces (2 of each).
  Cut 6 letters.
  Cut 6 shapes.

Felt

Cut 6 numbers.
Cut 6 letters with pinking shears.

Fusible fleece

Cut 6 animal faces.
Cut 6 squares each 3" (7.5 cm).

ASSEMBLY

With serrated knife, cut foam into 4 blocks each 5" (12.5 cm) square. Stitch 2 fabric squares together with $1/4$" (6 mm) seams, beginning and ending seams $1/4$" (6 mm) from each edge. Stitch 2 more squares in same manner to make a 4-square strip. Stitch remaining squares to either side of second square from one end of strip to make a cross. Begin and end stitching $1/4$" (6 mm) from each end. Stitch side seams. Place last square in position on top of cube and stitch 2 sides in place.

Turn right side out. Place foam inside block. Turn remaining seam allowances to wrong side and slip-stitch opening closed.

ANIMAL BLOCK

Following manufacturer's instructions, fuse an animal face to center of each of 6 large squares. Mark face details. With machine embroidery thread and appliqué foot, zigzag or use decorative stitches to outline each of the faces. Stitch face details with triple-straight-stitch along marked lines. Make machine eyelet eyes.

POCKET BLOCK

Fuse interfacing on wrong side of shapes. Zigzag marked side of each shape for opening. Pin a shape to center of each of 6 large squares. Zigzag remaining edges in place.

NUMBERED BLOCK

Following manufacturer's instructions, fuse a 3" (7.5 cm) square in diamond position on each of 6 larger squares. Zigzag the edges of the small square in place. Center and stitch the felt numbers to the diamonds.

LETTERED BLOCK

Trim fabric letters $1/8$" (3 mm) smaller than felt letters. Following manufacturer's instructions, fuse fabric letters to felt letters. Stitch to center of 6 larger squares.

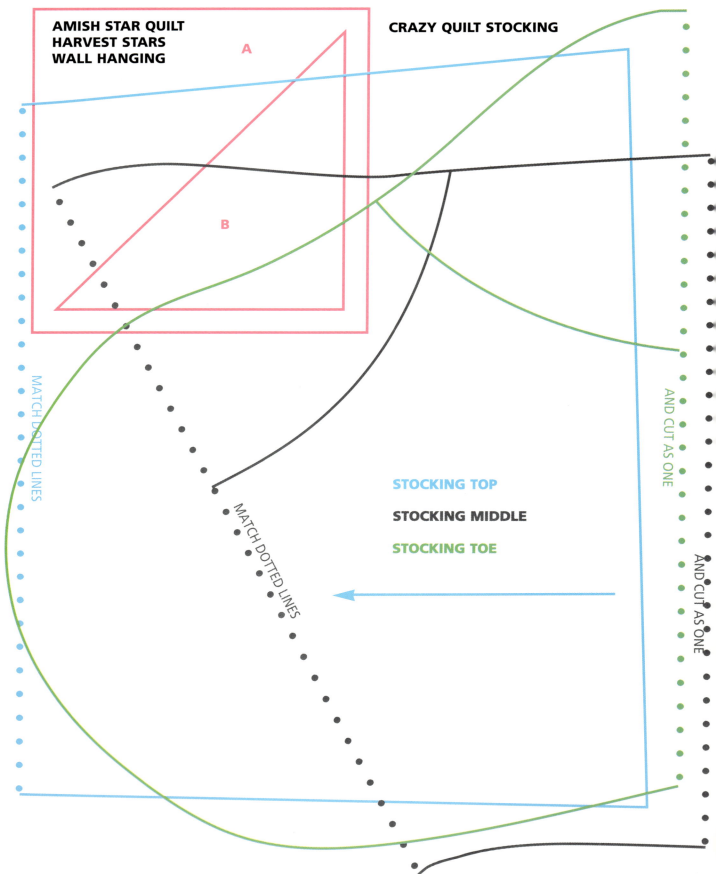

AMISH STAR QUILT
HARVEST STARS
WALL HANGING

CRAZY QUILT STOCKING

A

B

MATCH DOTTED LINES

MATCH DOTTED LINES

AND CUT AS ONE

AND CUT AS ONE

STOCKING TOP

STOCKING MIDDLE

STOCKING TOE

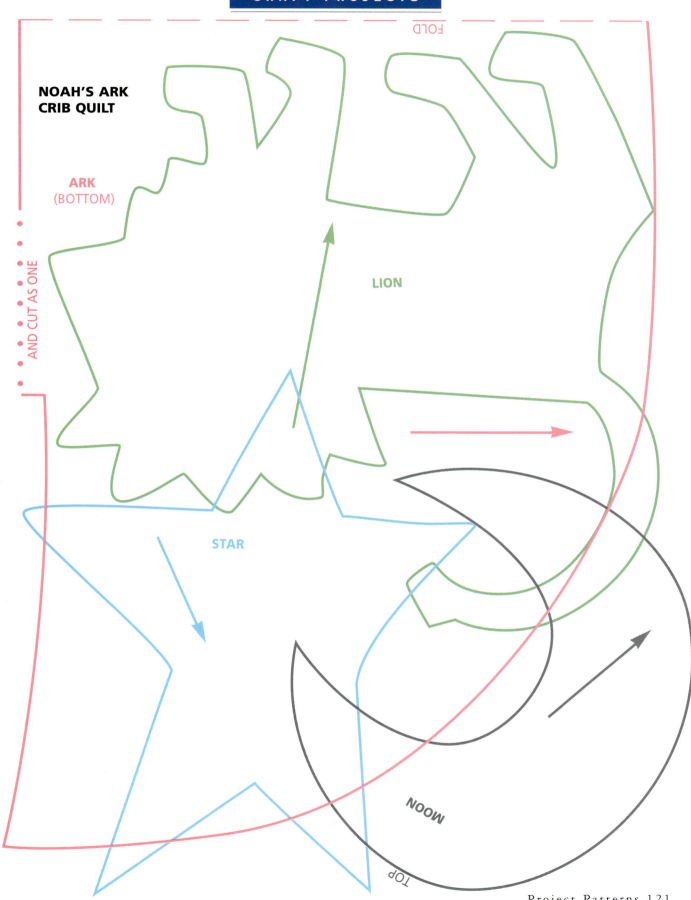

**NOAH'S ARK
CRIB QUILT**

ARK
(BOTTOM)

AND CUT AS ONE

FOLD

LION

STAR

MOON

TOP

**NOAH'S ARK
CRIB QUILT,**
CONT'D

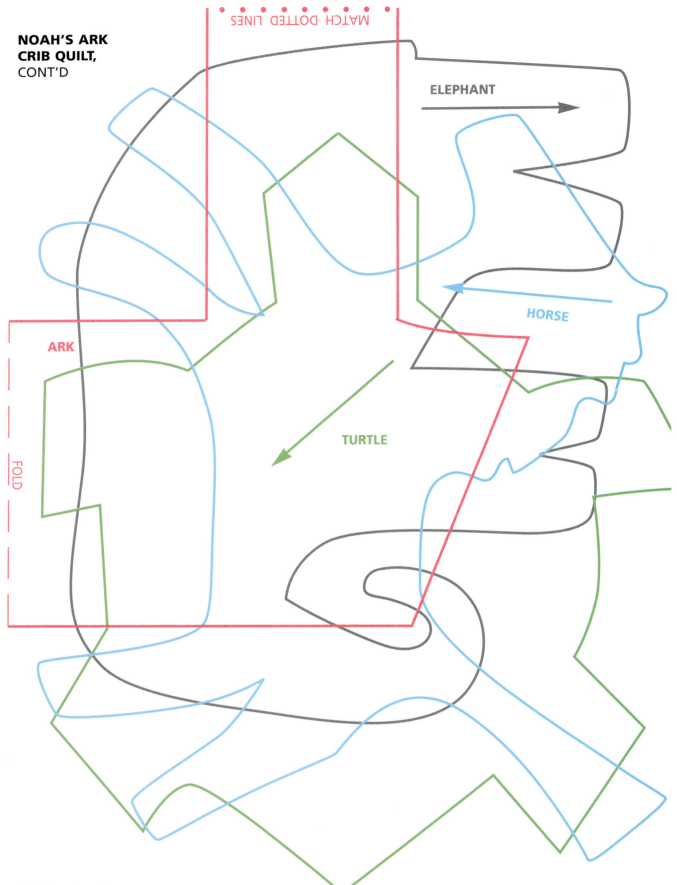

MATCH DOTTED LINES

ELEPHANT

HORSE

ARK

FOLD

TURTLE

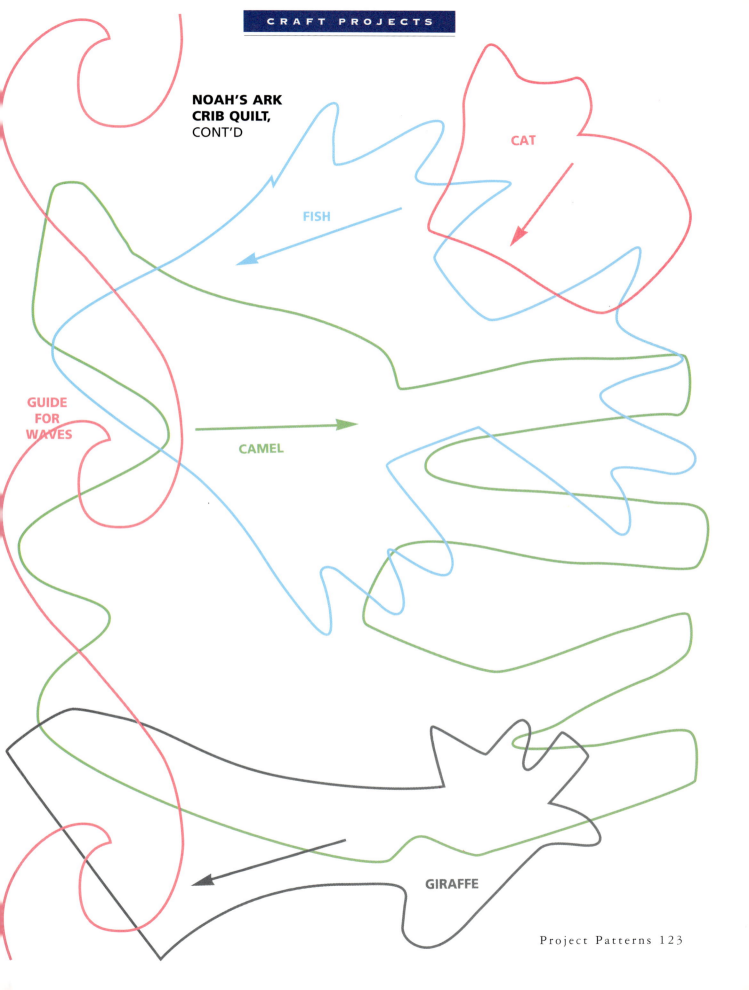

**NOAH'S ARK
CRIB QUILT,**
CONT'D

CAT

FISH

GUIDE
FOR
WAVES

CAMEL

GIRAFFE

SWEETHEART PILLOW

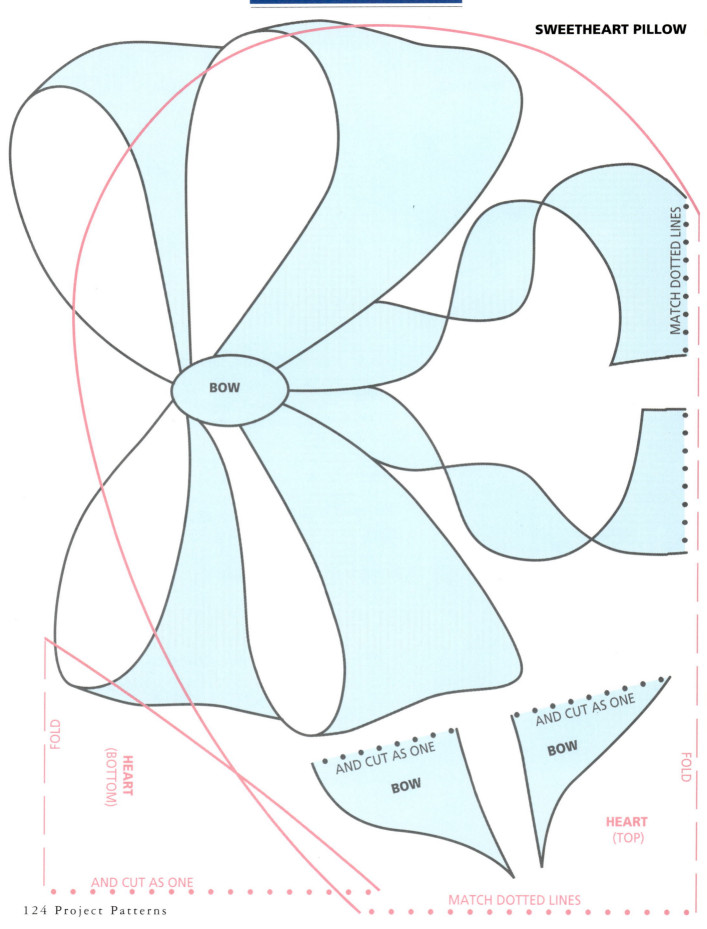

MATCH DOTTED LINES

FOLD

HEART
(BOTTOM)

AND CUT AS ONE

BOW

AND CUT AS ONE

BOW

AND CUT AS ONE

BOW

FOLD

HEART
(TOP)

MATCH DOTTED LINES

CLASSIC CUTWORK

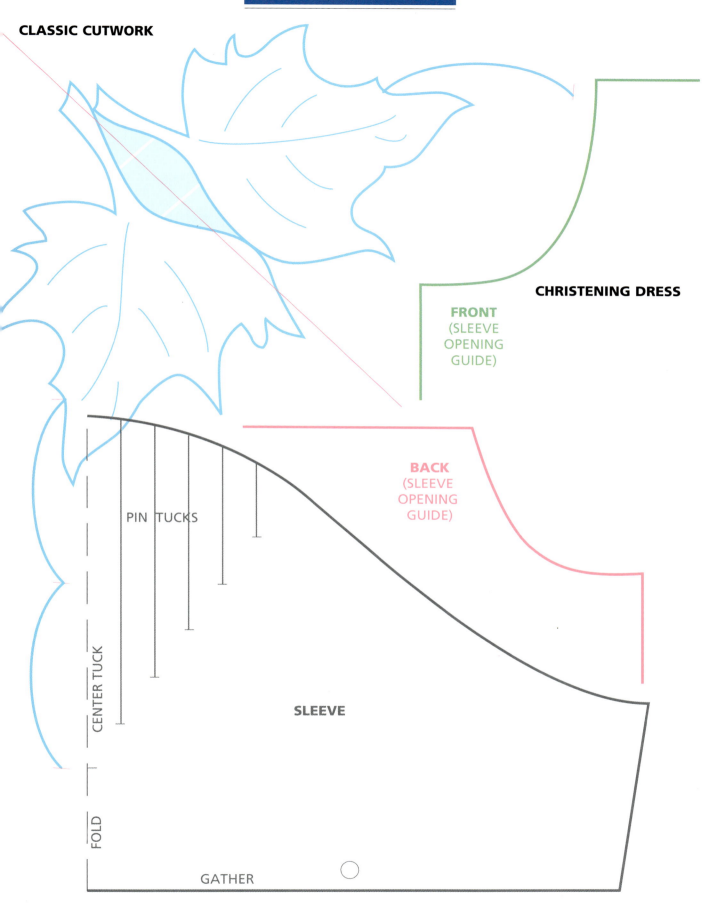

CHRISTENING DRESS

FRONT
(SLEEVE
OPENING
GUIDE)

BACK
(SLEEVE
OPENING
GUIDE)

PIN TUCKS

CENTER TUCK

FOLD

SLEEVE

GATHER

CHRISTENING DRESS,
CONT'D

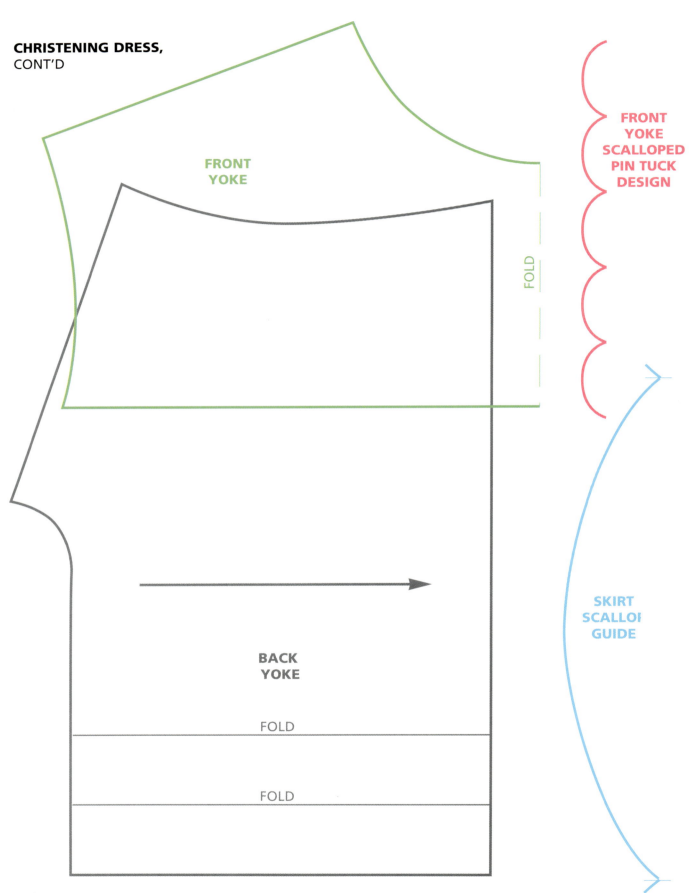

FRONT
YOKE

FOLD

FRONT
YOKE
SCALLOPED
PIN TUCK
DESIGN

SKIRT
SCALLOP
GUIDE

BACK
YOKE

FOLD

FOLD

**TREASURED MEMORIES
WALL HANGING**

TOPSY-TURVY DOLL

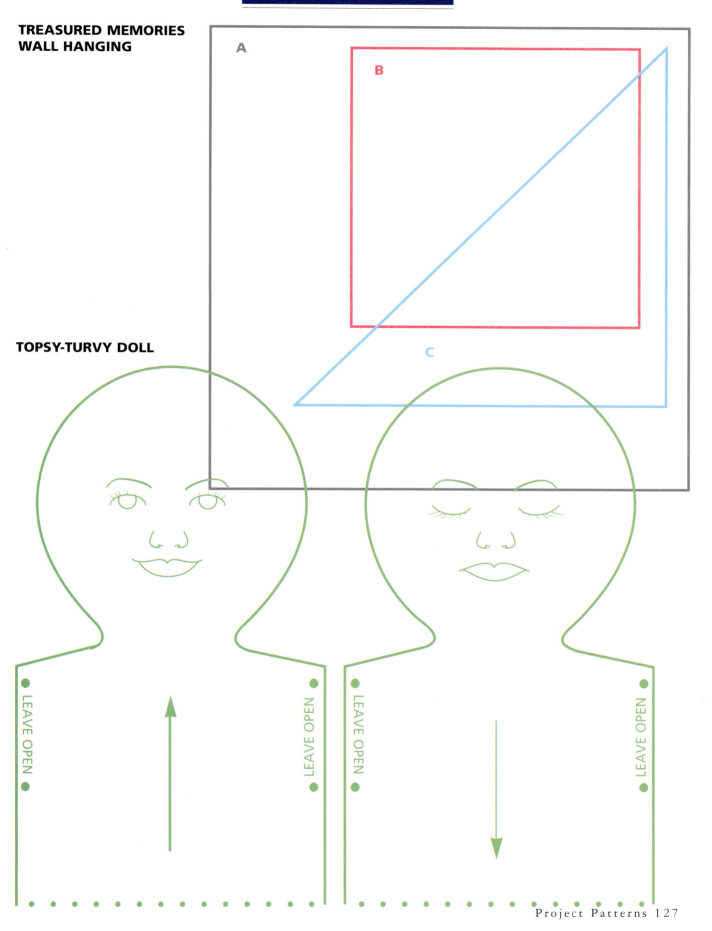

A

B

C

LEAVE OPEN

LEAVE OPEN

LEAVE OPEN

LEAVE OPEN

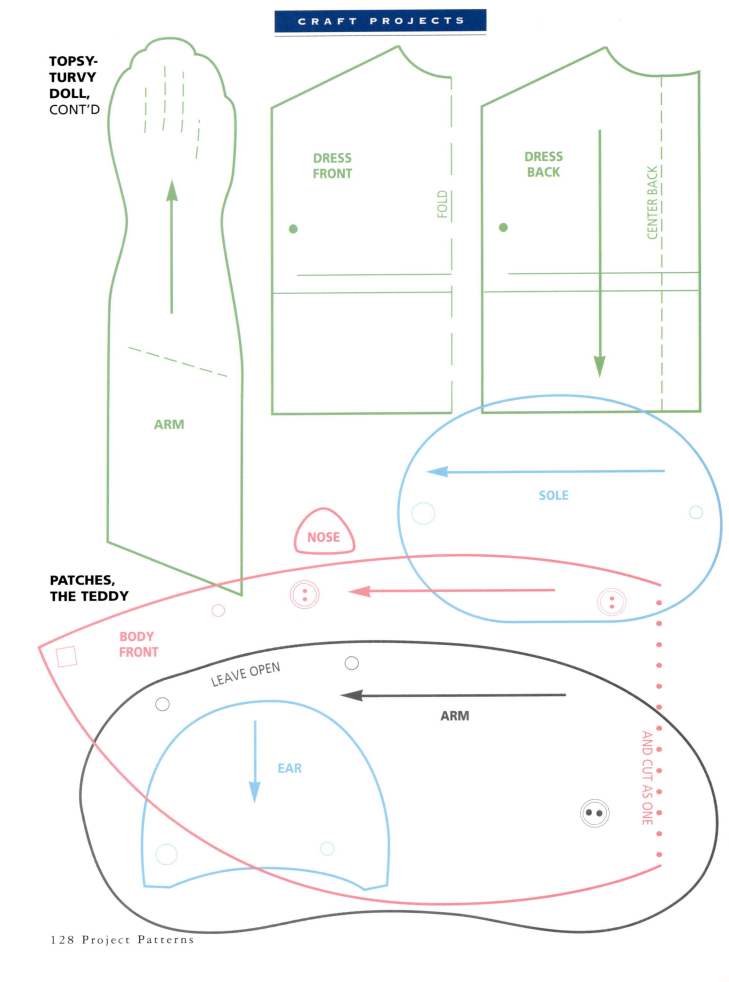

**TOPSY-
TURVY
DOLL,** CONT'D

ARM

DRESS
FRONT

FOLD

DRESS
BACK

CENTER BACK

SOLE

NOSE

**PATCHES,
THE TEDDY**

BODY
FRONT

LEAVE OPEN

ARM

EAR

AND CUT AS ONE

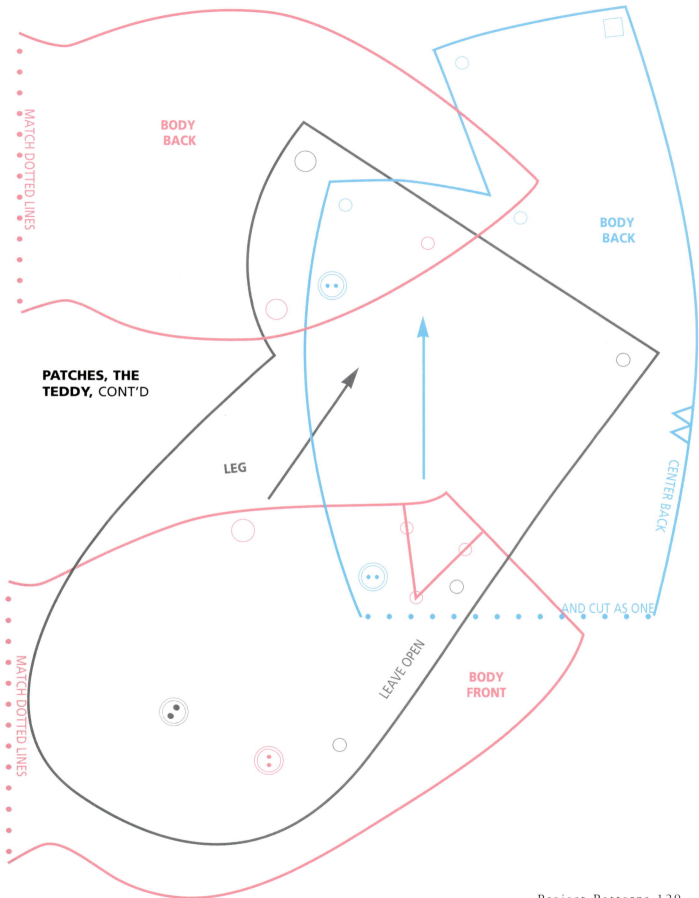

BODY
BACK

BODY
BACK

MATCH DOTTED LINES

**PATCHES, THE
TEDDY,** CONT'D

LEG

CENTER BACK

AND CUT AS ONE

LEAVE OPEN

BODY
FRONT

MATCH DOTTED LINES

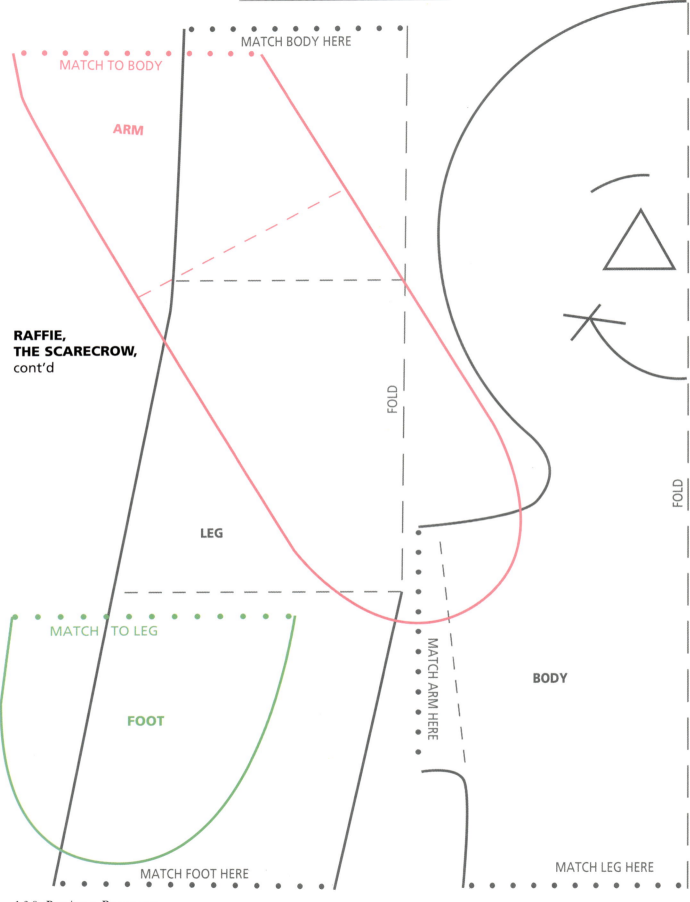

MATCH BODY HERE

MATCH TO BODY

ARM

RAFFIE,
THE SCARECROW,
cont'd

FOLD

FOLD

LEG

MATCH TO LEG

FOOT

MATCH ARM HERE

BODY

MATCH FOOT HERE

MATCH LEG HERE

RAFFIE, THE SCARECROW, CONT'D

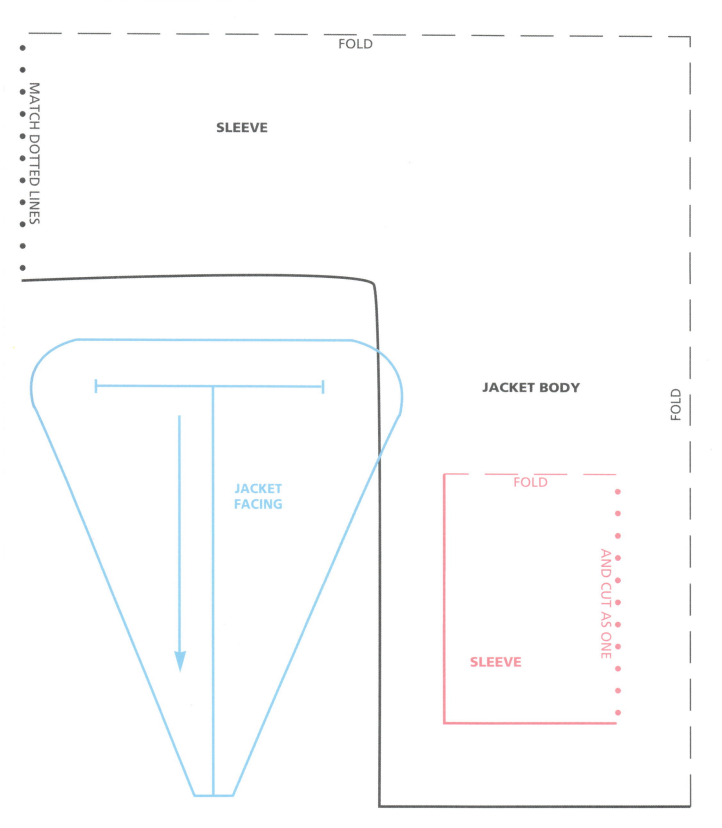

FOLD

MATCH DOTTED LINES

SLEEVE

JACKET BODY

FOLD

JACKET FACING

FOLD

SLEEVE

AND CUT AS ONE

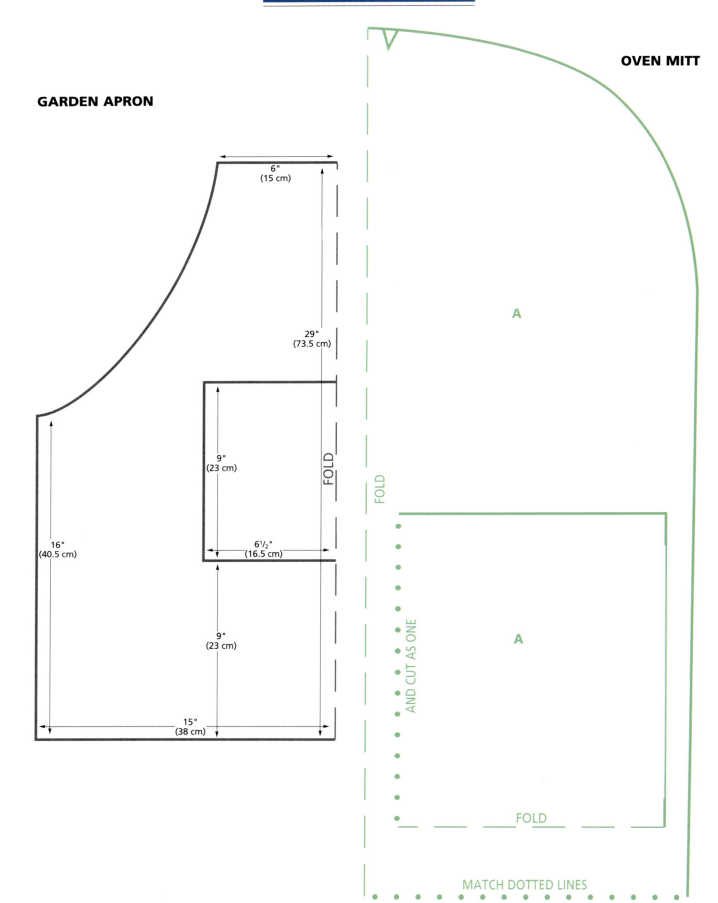

GARDEN APRON

OVEN MITT

6"
(15 cm)

29"
(73.5 cm)

FOLD

9"
(23 cm)

16"
(40.5 cm)

6¹/₂"
(16.5 cm)

9"
(23 cm)

15"
(38 cm)

A

FOLD

AND CUT AS ONE

A

FOLD

MATCH DOTTED LINES

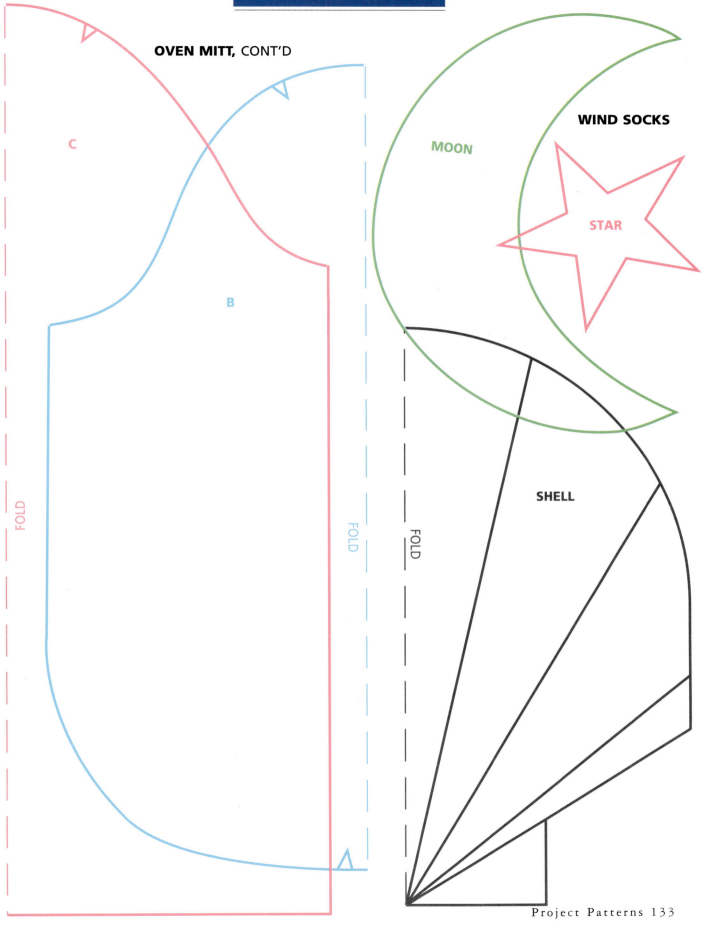

OVEN MITT, CONT'D

C

B

FOLD

FOLD

FOLD

MOON

WIND SOCKS

STAR

SHELL

WIND SOCKS, CONT'D

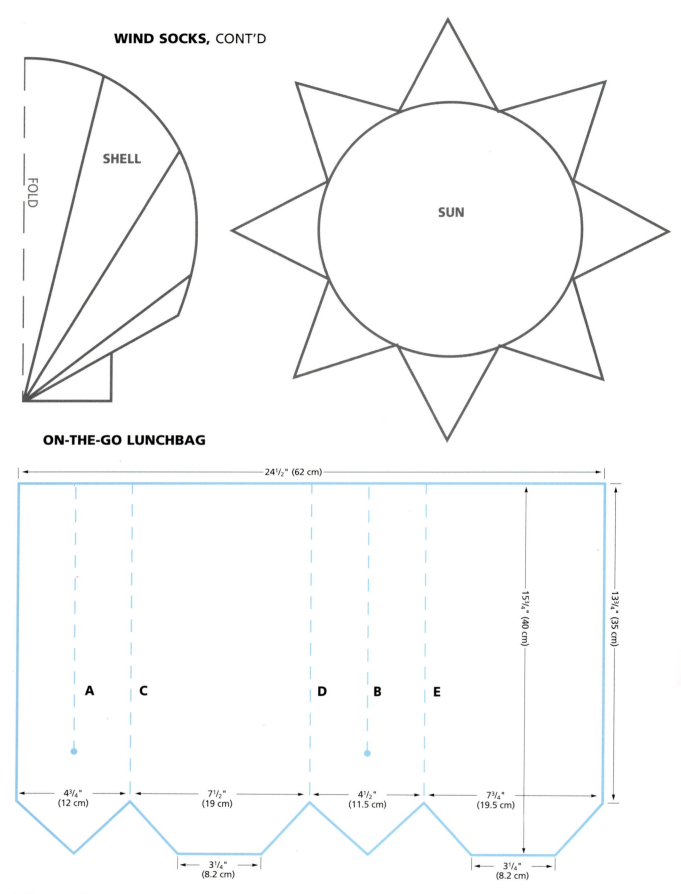

SHELL

FOLD

SUN

ON-THE-GO LUNCHBAG

24½" (62 cm)

15¾" (40 cm)

13¾" (35 cm)

A   **C**   **D**   **B**   **E**

4³/₄"
(12 cm)

7½"
(19 cm)

4½"
(11.5 cm)

7³/₄"
(19.5 cm)

3¼"
(8.2 cm)

3¼"
(8.2 cm)

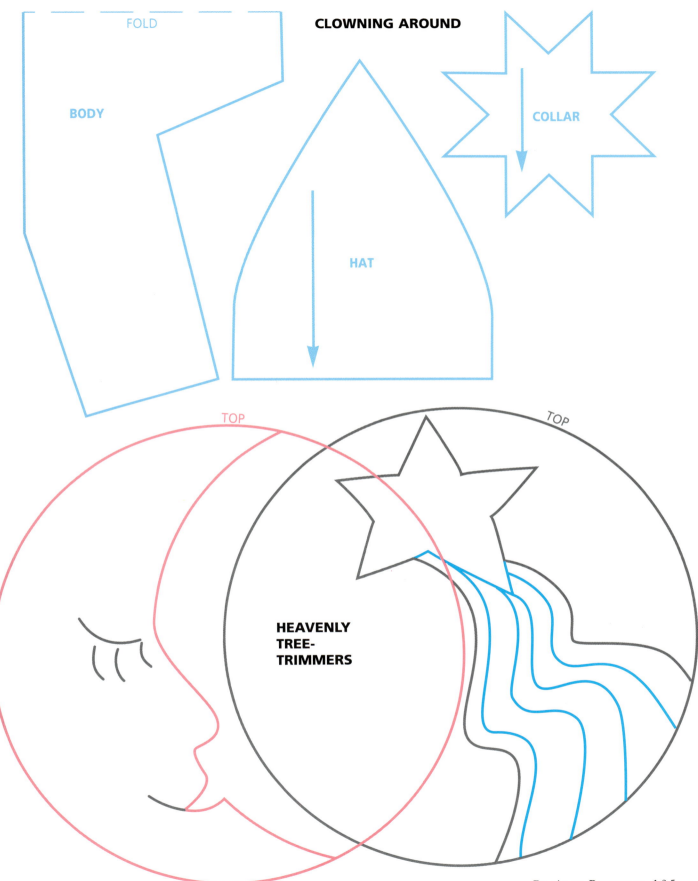

CLOWNING AROUND

FOLD

BODY

HAT

COLLAR

TOP

TOP

HEAVENLY TREE-TRIMMERS

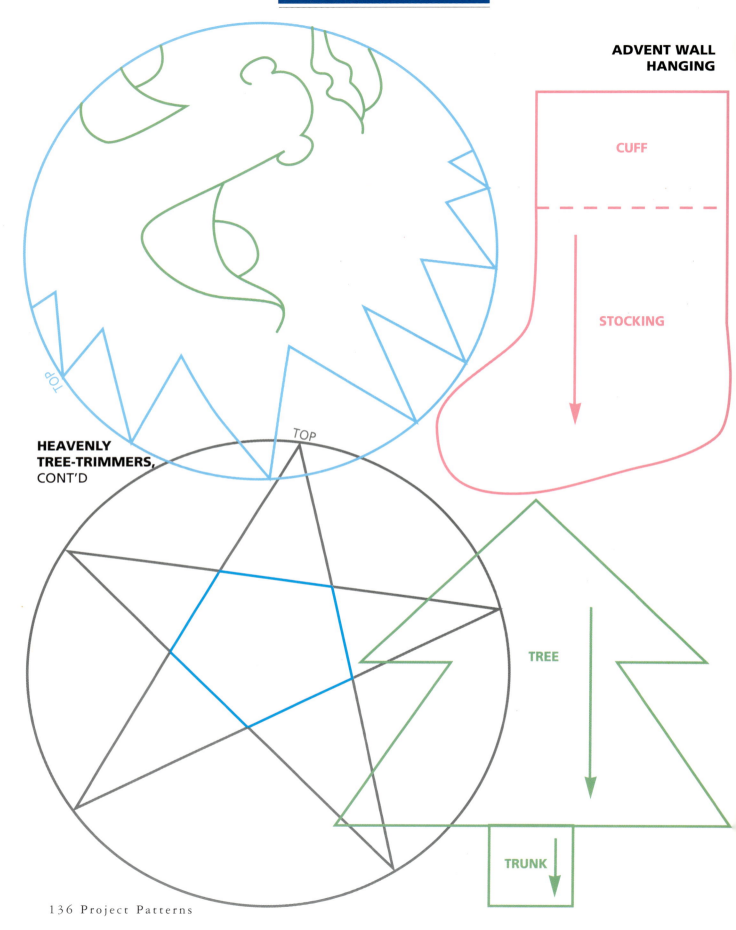

ADVENT WALL HANGING

CUFF

STOCKING

HEAVENLY TREE-TRIMMERS, CONT'D

TOP

TOP

TREE

TRUNK

APPLIQUÉD HAND TOWELS

BABY BLOCKS

LEAVE OPEN

**BABY
BLOCKS,**
CONT'D

BABY BLOCKS, CONT'D

LEAVE OPEN

LEAVE OPEN

BABY BLOCKS, CONT'D

Index

CRAFT PROJECTS

Acknowledgments

Project Designers and Samplemakers
Louise Baird, Julia Bernstein, Charlotte Biro, Linda Carr, Lila Chin, Gena Fausel, Gayle Hillert, Gurusurya Kaur Khalsa, Jill Krasner, Liza Prior Lucy, Crystal McDougald, Agnes Mercik, Bobbi Penniman, Joanne Raab, Patricia Richards, Helen Rose, and Jacquelyn Smyth

Special Thanks to
Linda Carr, Farrah Greenberg, Teresa Layman, Christina Mackell, Kathryn Nelson, Barbara Worton

Contributers
Sewing machines and sergers courtesy of Bernina of America

Thank you to the following companies: Coats & Clark, Dritz, Fiskars, HTC, Heat n Bond, Lion Ribbon, Mundial, C. M. Offray and Sons, Sulky of America, VIP Fabrics, Vogue Knitting, Waverly Fabrics

Photography
Photographers Andy Cohen, Lawrence E. Cohen, Frank Kuo
Photo Stylist Patricia O'Shaughnessy

Shot at Studio One Productions and the Waverly Showrooms

Styling Credits
Pottery Barn
700 Broadway
New York, NY 10003
Page 27 Candlesticks; Christmas ornaments, star and crackers
Page 43 Glass
Page 49 Tall glasses
Page 69 Red box
Page 112 Celestial ball

Treasures
95 Halls Road
Old Lyme, CT 06371
Page 52 Tray and vase
Page 100 Picnic basket
Page 102-103 Sewing basket
Page 116 Baskets
Page 118 Picture and basket

C.O. Bigelow Chemists, Inc.
414 Sixth Avenue
New York, NY 10011
Page 106 Hanging clown
Page 116 Bath oils and accessories

Paula Rubenstein Antiques
65 Prince Street
New York, NY 10013
Page 106 Vintage clown

Victoria Eckrich Antiques
88 E. 10th Street
New York, NY 10003
Pages 8-9 Table
Pages 18, 25 Shutters
Page 21 Watering can
Page 30 Vintage yarn ball
Pages 34-35 Fabric backdrop, paper bandbox, perfume bottle, and vintage frame
Page 43 Jewelry and tea set
Page 47 Vintage fabric, paper bandboxes and perfume bottles
Page 49 Boxes, glass vase
Page 52 Jewelry, and ceramic box
Pages 58-59 Table, map box, stool, cow, Mickey Mouse, clock toy
Page 73 Windmill toy
Page 86 Iron garden chair
Page 96 Crystal vase; assorted china
Page 118 Squirrel lamp

ABC Carpet and Home
888 Broadway
New York NY 10010
Page 30 Noah's Ark animals
Page 47 Needlepoint rug

Kate's Paperie
8 West 13th Street
New York, NY 10011
Pages 43, 74 Paper surfaces
Page 49 Book

Pattern Listing

For Sweet Sarah, page 66, we used Vogue Pattern #8336, designed by Linda Carr. Patterns to fit this doll are also available, as a series of wardrobe options. Refer to the Vogue Patterns Catalog for these designs.

Due to changes beyond our control, over time, this pattern may no longer be available. When this happens, call 1-800-766-3619 to order the pattern. Limited stock is kept for one year from the date the pattern is discontinued.

To order your free pattern, fill in the coupon on page 143. For further information, call Consumer Services, 1-800-766-2670.

FREE

VOGUE OR BUTTERICK PATTERN

To thank you for buying <u>Vogue & Butterick's Craft Projects</u>, we would like to send you a FREE Vogue or Butterick pattern of your choice.

Just fill in the coupon below and mail it to:

Vogue/Butterick Pattern Service
P.O. Box 549
Altoona, PA 16603

Canada:
Vogue/Butterick Pattern Service
P.O. Box 4001 Station A
Toronto, Ontario M5W 1H9

Offer open only to residents of the U.S. and Canada.

Vogue & Butterick FREE PATTERN OFFER
(Include $1.00 for postage and handling)

Please send me the following pattern:

❑ Vogue pattern   ❑ Butterick pattern

Pattern #_____ Size_____
                                        (If applicable)

Name _____
                         please print
Address _____

City _____ State _____ Zip _____

Allow 2-4 weeks for delivery. Offer good for all Vogue and Butterick Patterns except 1001 and 1002.

SS/CRA

ISBN: 0-671-88878-1
$17.00

For more sewing projects, look for the other Vogue & Butterick books featured on the Sewing Today television series:

ISBN: 0-671-88873-0
$17.00

ISBN: 0-671-88877-3
$17.00

AND COMING IN PAPERBACK FROM FIRESIDE IN SEPTEMBER 1994

The Vogue/Butterick Step-by-Step Guide to Sewing Techniques

An illustrated A-Z Sourcebook for Every Home Sewer

By the Editors of Vogue/Butterick Patterns

Featuring over 500 sewing techniques, each one thoroughly illustrated and arranged in alphabetical order for easy reference—from appliqués to zippers.